D1601345

MANAGEMENT
BY OBJECTIVES

MANAGEMENT BY OBJECTIVES

A System of
Managerial Leadership

GEORGE S. ODIORNE

Director, Bureau of Industrial Relations,
University of Michigan

PITMAN PUBLISHING CORPORATION

New York • Toronto • London

Eleventh printing   June, 1971

Copyright © 1965 by Pitman Publishing Corporation
Library of Congress Catalog Card Number: 65-18874
Manufactured in the United States of America
DESIGNED BY JEANETTE YOUNG

1.14   13   12   11

Preface

The appraisal of management performance has long been a subject of heated dispute.

The controversy has arisen because appraisals have traditionally been considered as a function separate and distinct from the general system of management itself. Yet the process of measuring managerial performance for the dual purpose of improving and rewarding it is not at all incidental to managing. It is manifestly part of the process of managing, and organizations in which managers are not measured are run quite differently from those in which the performance of the individual manager and the organization as a whole is measured against established goals.

The system of management by objectives is sometimes interpreted as a simple approach to conducting the "annual performance review" required by the personnel department. Such a view is usually symptomatic of a clash between a system for measuring and controlling performance, and a highly personalized, normally chaotic, mode of operation.

In this book the system of management by objectives is viewed in a larger context than that of a mere appraisal procedure. It regards appraisal as only one of the several sub-systems operating within the larger system of goal-oriented management.

It is also an underlying premise of this book that any system of management is better than no system at all. In defense of the system described here, however, let us hastily add that it incorporates most of the accepted major principles of management. Moreover, among its many advantages are vastly better appraisals of performance.

It should also be added that the system of management by objectives is not a technique that sounds reasonable enough in theory, but unfortunately hasn't been tried out yet. The author has personally observed it in operation in many successful organizations. He has studied literally thousands of statements of objectives set by operating managers. He has seen the system installed in many different kinds of companies over the past ten years, and he has assisted in subsequent evaluations of its effects.

The question may legitimately be asked, however: Is management by objectives really a *system?*

Purists in systems design will probably riffle quickly through the following pages and ask: "Where are the networks? Where are the 'three time estimates' of PERT? Where does probability analysis come in?" The answer is that there is nothing in management by objectives that excludes such sub-systems if the circumstances call for their use. A general system of management, however—if it is actually to be used by the majority of working managers to improve results —should not employ special sub-systems merely for the sake of being "systematic" in the esoteric sense of the word. In short:

• It shouldn't overcomplicate and oversophisticate the function of being a manager, but should try to simplify as much as possible a job that has become extremely laden with data, methods, and procedures.

• It shouldn't be dominated by its mechanics, or by recipes to be followed slavishly.

• It shouldn't be so philosophical and speculative that its effects are beyond measurement. Measurement of results is imperative because, ultimately, the economy itself imposes a crude but effective measure, namely profit, upon the business enterprise.

• It should be possible for line managers to use it without having to lean on staff specialists every step of the way.

• It should be reasonably self-regulating and self-operating rather than requiring heavy inputs of fear, control, or direction from a few on top upon the large number below.

Management by objectives is, in itself, not a complex system. Indeed it's the first requirement of such a system that it *simplify* and add meaning to overwhelming masses of information. How necessary this is for today's manager is all too evident from the jargon that assaults him on all sides—human relations, operations research, delegation, PERT, supportive management, discipline, linear programming, control organization, job evaluation, responsibility accounting, motivation, methods analysis, communications, value engineering, Theory X, Theory Y—and all the rest. Without a system that classifies and shows the input and output effects of these terms, it is impossible to make sense, let alone practical use, of all this material.

The major premises of management by objectives can be stated as follows:

A. Business management takes place within an economic system that provides the environmental situation for the individual firm. This environment, which has changed drastically over the past 30 years, imposes new requirements on companies and on individual managers.

B. Management by objectives is a way of managing aimed at meeting these new requirements. It presumes that the first step in management is to identify, by one means or another, the goals of the organization. All other management methods and sub-systems follow this preliminary step.

C. Once organizational goals have been identified, orderly procedures for distributing responsibilities among individual managers are set up in such a way that their combined efforts are directed toward achieving those goals.

D. Management by objectives assumes that managerial behavior is more important than manager personality, and that this behavior should be defined in terms of results measured against established goals, rather than in terms of common goals for all managers, or common methods of managing.

E. It also presumes that while participation is highly desirable in goal-setting and decision-making, its principal merit lies in its social and political values rather than in its effects on production, though even here it may have a favorable impact, and in any case seldom hurts.

F. It regards the successful manager as a manager of situations, most of which are best defined by identifying the purpose of the organization and the managerial behavior best calculated to achieve that purpose. This means that there is no one best pattern of management, since all management behavior is discriminatory, being related to specific goals and shaped by the larger economic system within which it operates.

As has been said, the author has observed at first hand the workings of management by objectives in numerous large organizations. At General Mills, a pioneer in the formal installation of this system, he obtained many valuable insights while serving as a member of the company's executive team. In various forms, it has long been used by General Motors, DuPont, General Electric, and numerous other leading corporations. Alfred P. Sloan was probably its major architect in corporate management.

The term, "Management by Objectives," first used by Peter Drucker in his *Practice of Management* (1954), has since become fairly well known. Douglas McGregor of M.I.T. and Rensis Likert of the University of Michigan have used it to justify the application of the findings of modern behavioral research to the business situation. While management by objectives does permit such an application, this is not a necessary condition for its effective operation.

Since 1960, the Bureau of Industrial Relations at the University of Michigan has conducted numerous seminars on this system of managing. The practical comments of the many participants in these seminars have been a proving ground for the materials in this book. Equally fruitful has been the experience gained by the author in serving as a consultant on the installation of management by objectives in such diverse organizations as Honeywell, Inc., Northwest Bancorporation, Dayton's, Minnesota and Ontario Paper Company, Northwestern National Life, J. L. Hudson, and T. Eaton Company of Canada. Executives from the Ford Motor Company, Detroit Edison, Parke Davis, National Bank of Detroit, and numerous other firms have also provided comment, sample sets of objectives, and other practical insights that have been incorporated in the following pages.

To all the executives who have shared in the making of this book through their advice, comments, and suggestions, the author extends his grateful appreciation. Especially germinal in his thinking has been his close working relationship in discussion, study, and co-instruction with Professor Earl Brooks of Cornell University, a genuine innovator in applying the system of management described here.

GEORGE S. ODIORNE

Ann Arbor, 1965

Contents

MANAGEMENT
BY OBJECTIVES

CHAPTER I

The New Look in Management

> *Every man who has acquired some un-*
> *usual skill enjoys exercising it until it has*
> *become a matter of course, or until he*
> *can no longer improve himself.*
> —BERTRAND RUSSELL

The old-fashioned capitalism of Adam Smith which flourished in this country throughout much of the nineteenth century is gone. In its place we have evolved what has been called "administered capitalism," which is an amalgam of classic capitalism and governmental control of private economic institutions. Most businesses have by now accommodated themselves to the new form of economic organization, and it is probable that no one seriously regrets the passing of the old-style capitalism, with its recurrent unemployment and widespread waste of human resources.

Nevertheless, man's long history has abundantly proved that in human affairs, as in the physical world, there is no gain without loss. Despite the indubitable advantages administered capitalism has conferred upon the many, there is no denying that it has resulted in a declining vitality in managerial leadership. It is the thesis of this book that, if the gains achieved by the new capitalism are to be sustained, let alone extended in the future, ways must be found to restore to corporate management the vitality and drive that characterized the old-time entrepreneur.

The Manager of Situations

What attributes are most likely to lead aspiring young men to success as corporation executives today? For more than four decades now, a small band of sociologists, led by Lloyd Warner of Michigan State University, has been studying this question.

The first conclusion these researchers have drawn is that ability counts more than social background. The second is that a college education is virtually essential. Of some 8,000 top managers studied, over 75 per cent attended college and almost 20 per cent had postgraduate education. The bulk of them, however, graduated from a handful of colleges—Yale, Harvard, Princeton, Illinois, Michigan, Chicago, Minnesota, California, Stanford, North Carolina, Texas, and New York University.

Yet it isn't certain that the managers of tomorrow will spring from the same roots as those of today. There is already some evidence that forces are at work that may alter the portrait of the corporate manager in the future. The youngster of today who simply imitates the educational pattern of a chairman of the board who was educated 40 years ago may find that the model has become outdated.

Men who achieved positions of power and influence in business during the Twenties were living in a very different world. For one thing, many more people are going to college today; and they are often from different backgrounds than the college students of a generation ago. In 1928, for example, only eight per cent of the sons of laborers went to college; by 1960, this proportion had risen to 34 per cent. This "upward mobility" is especially important when a young man advances beyond the bachelor's degree.

Some time ago, at the University of Michigan, we asked 105 company recruiters to identify the strongest candidates for management positions from those they interviewed in the placement office. We also asked them to tell us which ones they regarded as weakest in potential. The youngsters who were graduating with a master's degree rated nine to one better than the bachelor's candidates. One interesting sidelight was that, at the B.S. level, recruiters rated the sons of laborers lower, whereas at the M.A. level, they tended to ignore the question of social background. The advanced degree, which more and more students are acquiring, seems to be a definite means of breaking through to higher levels of management. The laborer's son graduating with only a bachelor's degree was less attractive to company recruiters, not primarily because of his background, but because he lacked, as the talent hunters put it, "the maturity, poise, personality, and appearance" needed to fit into the executive cadet corps.

A favorite game of college students is to pick the academic course most likely to lead to the top. Every time a controller steps into the presidency of a large firm (as has happened in the automobile business in recent years) students are sure to rush into accounting classes. Actually, of course, there is no one route up the ladder, and managers are just as likely to enter the executive suite from a side door.

Engineers who reach the top at an early age attribute their accomplishment to the engineering mentality they acquired at "good old Tech." Accountants, by and large, believe they can get to the top by starting with a CPA firm and then entering corporate life through the controller's office. Some very prominent firms are headed by lawyers who reached the top after having first acted as corporate counsel to their companies.

The electronics industry has its share of scientists who parlayed the brain power they applied to the creation of company products into the chief executive position. But at least two of the largest electronic firms, RCA and Westinghouse, have had chief executives who came from the management consulting firm that had been advising those companies on high-level matters. In other companies, the sales department is considered the best route; in still others, it is manufacturing.

What, then, leads to success in business? Does a formula actually exist?

First we might consider the Horatio Alger model for success— a formula which became popular in the latter half of the nineteenth century. The typical Alger hero was a poor, uneducated youngster who, by dedicating himself to the aims of his betters and adopting the basic virtues of nineteenth-century American morality, was able to rise through the ranks.

The Alger hero's success was measured by the steepness of his ascent. There was always a tremendous contrast between his humble origins and his final arrival into a world of tuxedo-clad men and bejeweled women in evening gowns attending operas, and attended by footmen, butlers, and an assortment of other servants.

The moral of the story was, of course, that a plucky and gritty youngster could begin as a shoeshine boy and eventually establish his own family dynasty. This happy arrangement linked the institutions of property and family with the equally laudable institution of equalitarian democracy.

It is true that much of America's economic growth can be attributed to family solidarity, which still contributes to the image of success in some ways. But, in practice, there is little similarity between the Horatio Alger model for worldly success and modern requirements for success in the business world. The owner-manager is a dying breed, and family ownership of industrial corporations has become an increasingly rare phenomenon. The new corporate managers who replaced the old-time "family capitalists" soon found it was neither natural nor appropriate to imitate the behavior patterns of their predecessors.

Managerial success became associated more and more with the performance of the corporation itself, and only incidentally with personal, off-the-job status symbols. The job became its own measure of success and high pay. Large but functional offices, the use of expense accounts, a company plane, and a company lodge became the ingredients attendant upon success.

Ultimately, the truth dawned on all but a few professional managers that there was no relation whatsoever between the old-time symbols of family capitalism—such as wearing an opera cape or having a chauffeur—and being a successful executive.

As organizational performance pushed aside the nineteenth-century concept of success, the Alger myth was shelved along with it. Rather than starting as a shoeshine boy who worked himself into the favor of the rich but kindly gentleman in the hansom, the new hero worked his way through Massachusetts Institute of Technology or the Wharton School; after graduating he was offered a job at $650 a month by company recruiters who interviewed him at the campus placement office. Once employed, his ascent through the organization was unrelated to his appreciation of fine wines.

Thus the new model for executive success became more complex and more diverse with the decline of family capitalism and the emergence of the managerial society. Joseph Schumpeter, perhaps the best theoretician of the new capitalism, emphasized the *productive* aspects of our new economic system as it emerged. He felt that productivity, engendered out of innovation under the aegis of the businessman, would bring about continuous economic growth. This in itself meant drastic changes in the accepted ideas of what the business leader looked like or, more appropriately, how he acted.

The new forms of creative leadership that accompanied these economic and social changes were gradual in coming. There was some delay before the literature of success pointed up a new formula for successful leadership. The formula was simple—that the creative leader must adapt his own, particular, personal qualities to the situation and to his followers.

Tangible changes in style, such as new fashions in cars, clothes, and even architecture, are immediately visible and readily accepted by most of us. That styles of management also change is less obvious. Nonetheless it is a fact of business life born of the pressures from the changing economic environment in which management is practiced. During the past 40 years we have lived through three distinct managerial styles: the "hard nose" manager of the 1920's and 1930's; the "human relator" of the 1940's and early 1950's; the "management by pressure" type of the late 1950's and early 1960's.

Let's look at each of these in turn, not simply to rehash the past but to single out some guides that will help managers define a model for the creative "manager of situations" of the future.

One of the most common articles of faith of older managers is the belief, "People don't want to work the way they did when I started out." This is partly true, and reflects the rigorous and often harsh standards that managers applied in directing work forces during the 1920's and 1930's. The labor force at that time was largely unskilled and unorganized. For the most part it was comprised of immigrants or first-generation Americans who accepted and, in fact, expected what we now regard as poor working conditions.

Many foremen, managers, and even company presidents handled their people in ways that seemed unduly strict or unfair. But the workers had to accept the situation because there were always others outside the plant gates only too ready to take over their jobs. Discipline was firmly enforced and the boss was most successful if he was tough. In such a climate, there was no need for managers to try to understand human relations and employee motivations. All they had to do to make workers follow orders was to hold over them the continual threat of firing.

With the advent of World War II the crowd outside the plant gate and the employment office shrank. As the war went on and the demand for workers increased, management practices in shop and the office had to change. Companies began to offer their employees more benefits and privileges and, for the first time, began worrying about how to keep them happy.

These measures were abetted by a wave of social scientists who entered industry expressly for the purpose of applying theories of human relations to the work situation. With pressing shortages of help in the face of a constantly expanding war effort, industry was sorely in need of the social scientists' advice. Essentially, that advice was: "Keep your employees contented and they will produce." This kind of thinking brought to the fore the manager adept at pleasing people, one who could maintain the euphoric atmosphere which was the background necessary for high production. Training courses emphasizing the ways in which managers could produce peace and harmony in the shop sprang up by the score.

In the late 1940's, another change of style became necessary. But this wasn't brought about by any new breakthroughs in social science. It was the result of a rising inflation which began to press harder and harder upon management and the economy in general. More and more companies began to discover that not all contented employees were productive and that it took more than a sunny atmosphere to turn out a good product and sell it. Characteristically, Claude Swank, vice president of manufacturing of Johnson and

Johnson told a reporter in 1951, "We've got to find some pegs to hang this human relations business onto so it will produce more, not just make people contented." During the early 1950's an increasing number of annual reports were noting that while sales volume was going up profits were going down.

By the end of the Korean war the cost-price squeeze was being felt by virtually all industries. This resulted in the development of a new style of *management by pressure* in which heavy pressure was exerted on the points where costs were getting out of line. This development brought about, in their turns, the hard line in labor relations, the expansion of industrial engineering departments, the improvement of systems and procedures, the introduction of the computer to cut office and paperwork costs, and the rise of the more action-oriented manager who could "make things happen."

In 1954, management expert Peter Drucker suggested that future managers would be held accountable for results rather than for the pattern of human relations within their plants and offices. He added, however, that managers should avoid exerting ungodly pressures upon the organization for results—that, in the long run, better results would be achieved by a more rational approach.

At any rate, the manager of the 1950's became a pressure expert, serving as a kind of human thermostat who turned the heat on and off the people below him. Management controls became a species of thumbscrew that enabled the top man to twist hardest in the right place for greatest effect. It once again became acceptable to fire people who hadn't produced. The fellow who could take the pressure and respond with good results moved up quickly.

Yet it wasn't a return to the "hard nose" days of the 1930's because there were still shortages of help in many areas. Despite the dips in the business cycle in 1953 and 1958, good men in many key areas were sufficiently scarce to require delicate handling. The trick was to exert enough pressure to keep people working harder, but not so hard that they would become discouraged and quit. So the human relations techniques learned in the 1940's came in even handier than before as the instrument of an all-out attack on what a well-known advertising man aptly called, "the age of the goof-off."

Thus the climate of the early 1960's set the stage for the development of the manager of the future—the *manager of situations*. This manager will differ from the pressure artist, the human relator, and the hard-nose of the past. Let us delineate those differences:

HE WILL BE JUDGED BY WHAT HIS FOLLOWERS DO

By definition, the leader is a person who has followers. Thus the quality of a manager is directly related to the quality of the men who work for him, and his own results are essentially those of his workers. Tomorrow's manager will be confronted with more complex technical and commercial problems than ever before. He won't be able to do all the work himself even if he should want to; he will thereby become more dependent upon good men working for him. If he has built an organization of pipsqueaks, as management development expert Jim Hayes of Duquesne University put it, "he's nothing more than chief pipsqueak." On the other hand, if he has pulled together a team of tigers, he is the head tiger.

HE WILL HAVE NO DEFINABLE "EXECUTIVE PERSONALITY"

The old game of trying to find the pattern of personality traits that distinguishes the successful executive is getting some critical attention. More companies are realizing that there is no point in trying to inculcate certain traits in people when all evidence shows that there is no single trait—or set of traits—always present in successful executives and always absent in unsuccessful ones. Appraisal systems and personality testing devices that aim at whittling away objectionable knobs on a man's personality or grafting new traits onto it simply do not work. This is not to say, of course, that habits and behavior cannot be altered for the better through training.

HE WILL MAKE THINGS HAPPEN

Nicholas Murray Butler, former president of Columbia University, once said that there were three kinds of people—those who make things happen, those who watch what goes on, and those who don't know what has happened. The manager of situations knows what is happening, and also helps to make things happen. It is he who decides that sales should increase, products developed, costs cut, or quality improved; and it is he who puts in the brains, the drive, and the leadership to bring these things about.

HE WILL BE MORE OF A GENERALIST THAN IN THE PAST

The manager of situations knows that he will be facing problems that go beyond any specialty. He is apt to be more adaptable and flexible than any specialist could possibly be. His expertise lies in analyzing situations, classifying problems, seeing causes, and identifying proper courses of action for others (who are specialists) rather than in being able to perform the work of his organization better than anyone else. He is more apt to be a creative thinker in unforeseen situations than an expert on familiar problems and areas of activity.

HE WILL BE AN ORGANIZER

Despite the dangers of conformity and stifled initiative that large organizations are reputed to have inherent in their structure, the use of management teams, task forces, and sound organization will increase. The very numbers of people involved, the specialization in some areas, and the growth of pressure groups for special interests will require the manager to exercise organizational skills. He will delegate more responsibility, but the vital point is that, after delegating details, he will spend more time studying and organizing the situation than he could if he himself attended to many of the lesser facets of the job.

HE WILL BE ORIENTED TOWARD RESULTS AND RESPONSIBILITY

These dual aspects of business life cannot easily be split into two distinct parts. Take for example the most common goals sought by the typical manager: profits and growth. In achieving these ends, the manager must take full responsibility for the means employed. He must operate within a value system. He cannot extract profits and growth from his business through unethical conduct; he must meet the ordinary standards of fair play and good citizenship. (One of the flaws of the management-by-pressure style of leadership was that occasionally the manager found that the pressure forced him into questionable paths.)

To sum up, the changing economic and social milieu has brought into existence a new type of manager. The ability to organize, get results, and adapt to rapidly changing circumstances will be the primary criterion for executive success in the future. The manager may be a specialist in his own field, but as manager he will use his analytical ability at the corporate helm, and he will allocate responsibilities among his subordinates. In short, the new manager will be truly a "captain" of industry.

The Competitive Situation

Since the 1950's, tougher domestic and foreign competition has made it essential for American firms to produce and sell with increasing vitality.

In this country there are 4.7 million business enterprises. Their average life span is seven years. Some 475,000 will expire this year and another 350,000 will change hands or become inactive. As a speaker at a recent business conference told his audience:

"Look to your left, and then to your right. Size up those two fellows. In all likelihood, one of you three will be out of business three years from now."

Be it remembered, though, that having freedom to fail, we also have the freedom to succeed and be rewarded for excellence. The crude reaction to competitive pressure of doing the same old things, only faster, has given way to more sophisticated strategies. The top manager of today knows that simply pouring out additional energy isn't sufficient. This energy and brain power must be directed toward the most productive uses if one is to come out on top.

Basically, meeting tougher business competition is a four-fold process:

- Identifying the kind of competition you're up against.
- Shaping your organization and plans to face it.
- Measuring progress against plans accurately.
- Reacting promptly to events.

IDENTIFYING THE COMPETITION

The first step is to size up accurately the nature of your competition. This is a complex process of watching both those who produce the same items as you do, and those who produce different but substitutable ones.

Thus, manufacturers of cans have to watch, not only one another, but also glass makers, plastics manufacturers, and aluminum fabricators.

When the consumer seeking to satisfy his recreational needs can choose between buying a color TV or a stereo or joining a book club, then the companies that produce or offer any of these alternatives must widen the scope of their attention to the potential range of competition.

COST AND PRICE COMPETITION. If several manufacturers offer identical products, the major determinant of success often lies in controlling and reducing costs to obtain the benefits of volume mass-marketing.

Internally this presses purchasing men, plant managers, industrial engineers, foremen, and office personnel into tighter cost-control and waste-elimination practices.

QUALITY COMPETITION. Another type of competition is provided by a product that is capable of performing in certain ways that other products cannot. This superiority may be due to the skill of the work force, excellence of equipment, meticulousness in design, or access to special materials.

The automobile industry, with its longer warranty on new cars, is typical. Quality of design and reliability in manufacture are important strategic factors in the auto makers' rivalry for markets. Styling, efficiency, and simplicity may be other special qualities that provide a competitive advantage. Such competition imposes great pressures on an entire organization, including research and development, engineering, manufacturing supervision, and sales and service.

TRADE ADVANTAGES. Local firms possessing inside information about local conditions or enjoying long-established business relationships and parochial loyalty comprise another kind of competition. The printing industry offers many examples. In this business, larger firms trying to gain new markets often find themselves beaten out by agile smaller plants accessible on the spot.

Faced with such competition, the bigger fellows may make a

play for the trade advantages of big orders and long runs, where bulk shipping costs and speed of production through high-investment equipment give them an edge.

Service industries are traditionally local businesses. Local contractors can often beat out larger national firms because they know the local laws and can sway the contracting principal toward favorite sons. A highly successful contractor in New York City might well be a terrible failure at building grain elevators in Montana, and, conversely, the fellow from Montana might not last a month in New York. Each knows his specialty and his own labor and economic environment; each can raise money from local bankers who know him—and know also that he runs less risk of making the big mistakes that would ruin an outsider.

BRAIN-POWER COMPETITION. One of the most expensive and most difficult forms of competition to overcome is that based on accumulated brain power—hired, trained, and encouraged to create.

It's said that eleven years were required for nylon to emerge from the laboratory in commercial form. In the computer-manufacturing business, the return to the company comes only after protracted periods of investment in brain power. It takes real financial strength and a history of strong profits to tool up for this kind of competition.

Having identified which of these four types of competition— or which combination of them—confronts it, the company can avoid sapping its strength in fields where its competitive disadvantages outweigh any possible strengths.

SHAPING THE ORGANIZATION

Simply identifying the competition isn't the whole battle. It's also vital that the respective parts of the organization be shaped into a unified team to take advantage of the company's strengths. "If you get your shot scattered you never hit anything," observes General Ed Rawlings, president of General Mills, Inc.

Focusing energies on a few tracks where the organization can run freely requires several kinds of managerial action:

FIGURE OUT WHAT KIND OF BUSINESS YOU'RE IN. The emphasis upon some proven lines of competence is an essential first step in the process of tightening up to compete better. The local firm with a strong position takes several hard looks at the dangers involved in going regional or national, where its local trade advantages no longer exist.

The chemical company walks cautiously around the temptation to jump into the electronics field. On the other hand, it doesn't hesitate to move strongly if it sees something which will strengthen its present position.

MOVE TOWARD GROWTH FIELDS. The Stanford Research Institute studies of what makes companies grow have shown that it's easier to operate successfully in a field expanding as a whole than in one that is shrinking. This means that the company that wants to remain competitive must keep its antenna up to identify which major lines are growing and which are dying.

Brunswick Corporation and American Machine and Foundry, which got into the bowling market early, grew because they saw a trend in its infancy. With an expanding population entering school, the publishing business became another growth field based on the same principle of watching areas with potential for new services or products. Age and population shifts, changing consumer tastes, and breakthroughs in technology are among the variables that must be considered in this orientation to fields which will grow.

HIRE GOOD NEW MEN AND MOVE THE BEST OLD ONES TO GROWTH LINES. College recruiting, hiring experienced men from other companies, lateral transfers of experienced and able men toward the spots where their efforts will produce the best return should all be part of the growth company's strategy.

In firms where marketing and advertising are the keys to competition, it's wise to recruit the best college men for marketing jobs. If it's research that's making the company move ahead fastest, then putting its best brains in the lab would be the sound strategic step.

Many companies have discovered that a sure trigger to high personnel turnover is to expose the best men to the frustrations of being a certain loser in competition. Not only does the excitement of new fields hold, but the sweet smell of success attracts the better men and makes the success-breeds-success pattern feed upon itself.

GIVE TOUGH MEN TOUGH GOALS. In a competitive business it's sound strategy to give tough-minded men the toughest problems. The able man will become abler, and the hard-driving man will become better skilled at overcoming obstacles if he finds himself pressed by the situation. This process follows a well-defined cycle:

Pick strong, resilient men to begin with and hand them high but attainable goals.

Get their commitment to the goal you'd like to see them achieve.

Watch each man's growth closely. If he seems to be stretching his capacity and can make goals easily which previously he found difficult, then raise the achievement level a little. He'll possibly groan, but he'll also grow to fit the demands upon him. Before long he'll be doing things that he himself thought he would never be able to do—and enjoying his new capacity to do them.

Don't make it easy for a man to fritter away his time once he's raised his capacity. Keep him taxed until you—and he—are convinced you've found his highest level of achievement.

John L. Handy, president of Handy Associates, a consulting firm, puts it this way, "It is indeed difficult to judge growth potential, but it can be done. No better test exists than to hand an executive business problems that are beyond his present level of responsibility."

Put a premium on new ideas, innovation and improvement in methods, products, processes, and projects. Simply administering or overseeing an operation doesn't help people fulfill their potential.

Instill a desire to excel in the whole organization, making the whole firm market, quality, and service-minded. This must include not only the sales force, but the clerks, machine operators, and staff people as well. The demand for excellence in every position is a vital part of pointing an organization toward more effective competition.

BE CREATIVE IN ADDING STAFF FUNCTIONS. One of the most important tools in meeting new competition is the strategic addition of staff people. In recent years a number of new and different staff functions have cropped up in growth companies. Some of these are unheard of in traditional organizations. Such positions as Director of Management Development, Director of Organization Planning,

Director of Commercial Development, Director of Market Research, and Research Production Coordinator are strictly modern in function and title. They reflect a basic, distinguishing change that has taken place in organization theory in almost all growth firms.

MEASURING PROGRESS AGAINST TARGETS

With the organization aligned to compete in the way that enables it to capitalize on its strengths and on the weaknesses in its competition, measuring progress against targets becomes the essential third step. Appraisals should not only measure a man but should also be closely tied to his unit's performance.

One large auto firm is presently installing a new appraisal system that goes beyond anything done along this line in the past. Not only is the effort and energy of the man rated, but this is equated against some specific measures of unit performance. Setting standards for managerial performance is pointless unless the performance of the manager's unit is measured too, this company believes.

The theory is simple. It presumes that many of the traditional ways of measuring managerial competence aren't germane. They merely check off a boss's rating of his subordinate's personality. The new emphasis in appraisals is to look over the man's shoulder and see what his followers have produced. If they have moved the organization along in competition with others, then the leadership of the unit is considered satisfactory. If the followers have not been effective, then the leader is considered responsible.

Thus, the measurement is applied to the manager's over-all results and not to his personality as rated by some abstract scale.

Adequate assurances against extraneous influences such as windfall profits or bad luck must also be considered in such evaluations, but even with these taken into account the major variables to be measured are results-against-responsibility-of-the-organization.

A manager's human relations skill, for example, is considered as one causal variable. If his results were bad because he couldn't apply the appropriate social sense to his task, he's rated low. This low rating isn't based upon poor human relations alone, but upon the bad effects it had upon results. This factor often takes more time to evaluate than a single accounting period. Some observers have proposed ten years as the period appropriate for the full working out of the values of an integrated system of sound human relations.

Even with such a long-term prospect of payback, there's some sense, many say, in preventing the short-term opportunist from wringing too much from an organization for a short period at the expense of future productivity and growth.

Thus, while measurements count results, they need to be more than simple cost-accounting procedures. Rather, they consist of economic measurement over the growth cycle of a firm. Such measurements would include evidence of attracting and keeping high-potential young men, and averting the loss of experienced men with ideas and energy.

REACTING PROMPTLY TO EVENTS

A distinct characteristic of the new strategy for meeting competition is the development of people and procedures for reacting quickly and intelligently to earlier results. This means that market advantages are exploited quickly as they occur, and that special evidence of talent or leadership is sought out as it appears in the day-to-day rush to get the job done.

In one company, a list of the young executives with great potential is compiled annually and special developmental assignments and tougher jobs await those who get aboard this roster. It isn't, however, a "Crown Prince" list to which a man is assigned permanently or forever barred. It is grounded upon continued performance, and those who rest too easily on past laurels may find themselves unseated by more up-and-coming late-bloomers.

This tactic of reaction to new events calls for suitable responses to new and different conditions, either to take advantage of them, or to avert the setbacks that could result from unbending compliance with a plan suddenly outmoded.

Management policy, suggests Sun Chemical Company executive William Machaver, should be considered as having a life of five years or less, subject at that time either to renewal or revision as the new climate may indicate. A somewhat shorter period is desirable, however, for the gestation and life span of a procedure. Specific programs should be prepared for a year in advance, with subordinate sections of the program set for time periods measured in months.

Why is there constant turmoil in changing short-run objectives? Primarily, this is due to the results of previous programs themselves, which dictate the actions of the next phase. For the most part, the continuity over time will be constant, with change growing out of new competitive attacks and the actions of competitors. Hence, long-range plans are most valuable when they are revised and adjusted and set anew at shorter periods. The five-year plan is reconstructed each year in turn for the following five years. The soundest basis for this change is accurate measurement of the results of the first year's experience with the plan against the targets of the plan.

As business competition increases, the growing interest in strategies of competition—including such new mathematical methods as game theory, plus the accumulated know-how of practiced campaigners—may be expected to make the business struggle more sophisticated than in the past. It is likely that staff experts who specialize in competitive strategy will increase in importance. Such functions as commercial development departments, organization planning departments, and market research groups are perhaps a precursor of the more elaborate methods companies will use to meet the tougher new competition which awaits them in the next two decades.

Ends vs. Means in Modern Management

Today's corporate managers are caught on the horns of a dilemma. On the one hand they must show a profit, and on the other they are obliged to provide a high level of well-being for their employees and confine their business practices to the commonly accepted ethical standards of the society in which they operate. These often-conflicting pressures have had profound effects on American corporations and on the men who manage them.

Not long ago I spotted a copy of Machiavelli's *The Prince* lying on the work table of a company president. "Sort of a joke one of our management consultants is playing on me," the executive explained, on noting my inquiring gaze. "He said he was going to send me a book on how to work out the problem of results, and how to get them."

This man's consultant may have been more practical than he realized, for the same problem that concerned Machiavelli—the relation of means to ends—has caught today's management in a vise. On the one hand there is the pressure to achieve results. On the other there are counterpressures to limit the means employed to certain socially and culturally acceptable methods. In fact, three distinct kinds of pressure systems are now building up in American management: mounting pressures for lower costs, higher profits, and greater efficiency; new pressures for more advanced personnel policies, some of which add to costs; a new puritanical attitude toward advertising, antitrust, and conflicts of interest on the part of corporate officers.

Since these three pressures are seldom wholly compatible, the job of managing a large firm today involves a great deal of tension. This can be clearly seen if we examine each of these areas of pressure more closely.

THE COST-PRICE SQUEEZE

Because stockholders and directors have been watching their company's profits slowly shrink, they have been putting considerable pressure on managers to match growing sales volumes with higher rates of profit. But, at the same time, the brief return of price and wage controls in certain areas during the Korean war brought on a general consumer revolt against inflation. No longer do customers accept price increases without protest. Consequently, managers are caught in a "cost-price squeeze."

In an effort to slip out of this squeeze, managers have taken a renewed interest in competition on a price basis. Salesmen are exhorted to be more aggressive and not to be content to function as mere "order takers." Industrial engineers armed with methods programs, value analysis plans, and automation proposals swarm over factories seeking to eliminate pennies of unit cost. Purchasing men, tax experts, labor negotiators, cost accountants, and personnel men all struggle to trim off "organizational fat."

The search for new products has caused research and development expenditures to zoom to an estimated $20 billion this year, compared with a meager $400 million in 1940. Electronics experts are wiping out complete divisions of clerks and accountants through the introduction of data-processing systems. Hard-sell advertising is again in vogue. In some instances, the ravages of cut-throat competition have led distracted marketing managers into some unwise attempts to collaborate with competitors in order to "stabilize certain markets."

One result of all this is that managers are now promoted and rewarded on the basis of the results they have been able to achieve rather than on the extent to which they are able to match some psychologist's profile. Bonuses, bigger jobs, and stock options are thrust upon the man who makes things happen and gets results.

A further consequence has been to make the profit motive more respectable. Businessmen are keenly aware of the need for profit for the sake of economic growth and the maintenance of our competitive position in the world—to say nothing of full employment. Top government officials are also keenly aware of the impact of declining corporate profits on the national budget.

Even labor leaders are relatively more tolerant of what they might have damned as exploitation ten years ago. Former Secretary of Labor Arthur Goldberg, in a recent interview, told a national TV audience that the government, the public, and labor all have a stake in the continued profitability of our private enterprise system. Admittedly, the labor leaders don't make business profitability a primary aim of unionism, but their present tolerance toward profit represents quite a change of heart.

HUMAN RELATIONS PRESSURES

But while management is off on a pell-mell race to protect the profit margins of business, it must also contend with the widespread movement toward improved human relations in industry. For the most part, the philosophy prevalent during World War II that a "contented worker is a productive worker" (which Daniel Bell once described as "cow sociology") has been shelved in favor of harder work and discipline on the job. But despite the introduction of more rigorous standards of employee performance, the question of the proper "care and feeding" of employees is still a headache for managers and a source of pressure upon costs.

True, harder bargaining in labor negotiations in an effort to control costs has characterized the new climate of contract negotiations. Also, firmer discipline and tighter social and technical organization of hourly rated workers seems to be firmly established. But the number of unskilled workers is on the decline, and the human relations problem still remains for such expanding segments of the work force as clerks, service employees, and engineers and scientists. Pressure to achieve improved personnel relations grows rapidly in the modern corporation, and several approaches to this end have been tried.

First of all, over the past few years the pressure to achieve better human relations has brought about a change in the pay package, which now includes not only wages and salaries, but also such fringe benefits as pensions, insurance, and supplemental unemployment and sickness benefits. This trend toward tax-saving but permanent fringe benefits alarms many managers. Often they give in reluctantly to demands for such benefits, feeling at heart that by doing so they may be prevented from reaching their primary goal.

Secondly, influential opinion makers, especially the university social science departments, are putting pressure on managers by espousing basic changes in styles of company leadership. But many social scientists usually propose methods untested for their long-run effectiveness in reducing costs. The scholar is often frankly experimental in his approach to human relations. The executive knows pragmatically that he must make a leadership style work profitably for his firm, long after the social scientist has returned to the campus.

Extensive research reports, usually on studies conducted in unidentified firms, have indicated that softer management approaches are more efficacious than traditional methods. Unable either to accept these reports fully, or to reject them out of hand, many managers are uneasy about which style of leadership to follow. As one company president said:

> I read about the experiments in human relations advocated by social scientists, but I wonder about them. All too often they don't mention the firms that conducted the experiments, so I can't go and talk to their executives. In some cases, when I have

found out the names of the firms involved, I have heard conflicting stories about the actual results. The thing I can't really
decide is how true the accusations are that a lot of the social
science research results have a built-in bias in favor of participation for its own sake, rather than being complete objective
reports of all the significant facts.

A personnel research man for a large electric company is even
more candid. A Ph.D. himself, he said:

> I've followed up on a lot of social science studies conducted
> in such places as General Mills, Prudential Insurance, and Gen-
> eral Motors, and I find that the working executives in many of
> these companies are eager to fill me in on gaps in information
> which sometimes explain the results in totally different terms
> than those presented by the researchers.

But a gnawing suspicion lingers that perhaps the social scientists are right; and the possible long-run effects of rejecting their
findings bothers many executives and leaves them hesitant either to
move vigorously ahead with their own policies or to adopt new ones
wholeheartedly.

Still another area of human relations which is growing rapidly
is that which has to do with the employment of people ordinarily
considered unemployable. Such groups as the physically handicapped, the mentally retarded, older workers, school dropouts,
minority groups, veterans, the blind, and those with criminal
records all have their own proponents interceding with employers
on their behalf.

As the personnel manager of an auto firm in the Midwest
reported:

> Not a day goes by without a visit by one of these committees,
> urging me to hire more older, younger, physically handicapped,
> or otherwise marginal members of the labor market. Our man-
> agement wants to do the right thing, but we also get some
> hellish pressure from our Detroit office for results, and it takes
> plenty of doing to try to fit some of these people into our or-
> ganization and still run at a profit.

Still another executive stated:

> I wish I could find a couple of talented college graduates with
> MBA's in accounting or finance who are also Negroes. I have a

committee which is pressing me to get some colored professionals in our accounting department, but I can't find good
accountants of any kind. I would certainly be relieved if you
could refer to me a bright young colored man or woman who
could meet our standards for accounting trainee.

The genuine desire of men of good will in management positions to perform such socially desirable acts runs into a barrier that
is more formidable than prejudice or callousness on their part. It is
the pressure to keep their firm from being deluged by a wave of
rising costs, which could wipe out the jobs of all.

THE NEW PURITANISM

Coupled with the new human relations offensive is a drive for
"hound's tooth" cleanliness in the marketplace. Such a drive can
have direct and immediate effects on business by reducing profits,
raising costs, or cutting sales. The new puritanism has many facets.

First of all, it has made itself felt in television, which is the
major medium through which most products are now brought to
the attention of consumers. Newton N. Minow, former chairman of
the Federal Communications Commission, has described TV as a
"wasteland," a form of escapist entertainment riddled with sex and
violence which is forced into the home in the interests of increasing
sales. But mass marketing seems imperative to managers who want
to keep their plants running, let alone provide jobs for all the unemployed unemployables being urged upon them by private committees and by the government.

As one executive described it:

> Recently I went to Washington and visited the White House
> to sign the pledge that we would abide by the Fair Employment
> Practices Committee code. While I was in Washington I also
> testified before the FCC and defended myself and my company
> against attacks upon the quality of a TV program we sponsor,
> which is selling cars to beat the band. It seemed strange to me
> that nobody at either event seemed to see any inconsistency
> in what they were doing.

Norman Strouse, president of the J. Walter Thompson advertising agency, told the Advertising Club of San Francisco that the new
puritanical attitude toward TV and the advertising industry was not

only preventing business from doing its job as well as it should, but would also, if it continued, probably lower our standard of living.

Another facet of the new puritanism is tougher antitrust enforcement. The recent jail sentences meted out to the executives of electrical companies who conspired to fix prices have placed industry under severe pressure to avoid all kinds of actions that might further damage its public image. The case of the electrical conspiracy provides a clear example of the conflicting forces pressing upon today's executive. Since some heavy electrical equipment was being sold below cost, the conspirators found that only through collaboration could they protect the earnings of their firms.

They conspired because they felt the pressure for results more strongly than they felt the pressure to remain spotless in the eyes of the law. Business conferences with their superiors were more apt to be "sweat sessions" over profits than discussions of how to comply with the letter of the law. Being mortal, they succumbed to the greater pressure.

In another industry, a recently retired president said:

> I'm glad I could retire today. Ten years ago, when this business was losing money because of cut-throat competition, I finally got most of the big guys together and we agreed to stabilize prices. As a result, we had a long breathing spell wherein we could make a decent profit and grow. We doubled our plant and work force, and paid for some good research during that period. The new president—poor guy—has another situation. He's under more pressure to produce profit, but with the way the antitrust people are watching us, he doesn't dare work out any arrangements to stabilize things the way I did. As a result, in order to keep the plant running, his salesmen are taking orders they know will lose them money. This can't go on. Something will have to give eventually.

Actually, many managers find that the conflict between ends and means is essentially one of conflict between two desirable ends. The first is keeping the company healthy; the second is living up to the values of the environment in which it functions.

As a result of the interplay between these pressures and counterpressures, a new picture of management goals seems to be emerging. This picture has three dimensions:

Profit

Once a matter to be explained apologetically and self-consciously to outsiders, however vigorously sought privately, profit is now more respectable than ever.

Growth

The need to provide jobs and meet competition has underlined the importance of constant expansion, reinvested earnings, and innovation in products, methods, and markets.

Survival

The realization that certain value systems must be adhered to has altered management's outlook and behavior, and has resulted in tighter internal controls, more public relations efforts, better communications, and an increase in community service programs.

This trio of objectives, as one executive pointed out, is "like the famous billiard balls of Alfred Marshall" in that, if one is moved, the other two are affected. Profit, for instance, must now be extended beyond the accountant's definition to include many of those indirect expenses that insure growth and survival. Expenditures for personnel management, management training, public relations, and community, educational, and research projects become legitimate management objectives since these actions contribute to the growth and survival of the corporation in today's pressure-laden world.

A far cry from the simple economic model of Adam Smith, today's corporate system has adapted to the complex world of the sixties. In the past, public relations, human relations, and government relations were often given mere lip service by many managements. But threats of bankruptcy and dissolution have changed token allegiance into firm conviction.

It is probable that corporations will, in the future, make far more than mechanical gestures toward service to the surrounding community. Like profit and expansion, such service has become a primary target of management. It must now be programmed into future operations, thus becoming part of the real standards by which managerial success is measured.

CHAPTER 2

A Flight
from Capitalism?

> *The scheme of values of capitalist society, though causally related to economic success, is losing its hold, not only upon the public mind, but also upon the capitalist stratum itself.*
>
> —JOSEPH A. SCHUMPETER

The search for an appropriate style of management and leadership has often been muddied by some assumptions of modern behavioral-science students of management. These assumptions have been rooted in the philosophy that the proper style of management is completely determined in advance by the nature of the manager's behavior.

Modern science—and modern management—assumes, however, that the existence or suitability of a particular style of management always depends upon the mutual relations of a number of physical and social factors, the behavior of the manager being but one of them. This doesn't mean that the nature of the manager and his behavior are insignificant. It means that the situation assumes as much importance as the manager and his behavior.

In the previous chapter we pointed out that changing situa

tional factors led to successive changes in style of management. From this phenomenon it should be evident that understanding the situation in which management must function is as important as understanding management methods and skills themselves.

If the manager is to "understand the situation," he must have a broad insight into the human condition in today's world. To provide that insight would be an over-ambitious project for a single book, and would in any case divert us from the purpose of this one. Nevertheless, there are certain pertinent facts in the modern business situation that must be noted if we are to understand how a system of management can function effectively, or even to justify the proposition that it is feasible at all.

In the following pages we shall consider certain factors in what can be described as the larger system within which a manager must operate. As we shall see, these factors point to the conclusion that, possibly for a decade or more ahead, the appropriate system of management will be one that is goal oriented and measures performance by results.

Just why this is so—and what will happen if managers fail to operate in this manner—will be discussed in this and the following chapter. The literal-minded reader who is more interested in knowing how to manage than in understanding why a particular technique should be used can skip to Chapter Four if he chooses. Here, as has been said, we shall be concerned simply with the reasons why management by goals and results is imperative for the manager of the modern corporation.

Business began its retreat from old-style capitalism in earnest in 1931 and formally capitulated in 1952. The nation's confidence in capitalism, which had stood firm for seventy years, was rocked by the Great Depression in 1931. With the election of Eisenhower in 1952, an acknowledged conservative was established at the helm, where he could administer, consolidate—and permanently establish —the liberal reforms of the previous two decades.

Ups and downs in the business cycle had not been unknown before 1929. In fact, one-third of the time since 1820, the rapidly expanding economy of America had been depressed. Each ride down the sloping side of a business cycle had brought business failures and unemployment for the duration of the slump. Each time the economy had weathered the decline and risen to new heights. Frightening as the declines might have been, and certainly uncomfortable to those who lost jobs or businesses, the recurrence of crises from time to time never shook the basic reliance on risk taking as being best for all.

The depression changed all this. Roosevelt's New Deal represented the proposition that risk could be reduced or even eliminated altogether. After his sweeping victory at the polls, Roosevelt began immediately to unite the nation into a "great organic entity." He saw the presidency first as a position of moral and social leadership, in which the tools of economics were used as demanded by the social dictates of the people at large. If he had any economic philosophy it was welfare economics, which has been defined as being "concerned with the means by which economic activity can be made to contribute most fully to the social well-being."

In his first hundred days of dealing with the Congress, Roosevelt proposed and secured more sweeping controls over the economic affairs of the nation than any president had except during wartimes. Agencies for central planning staffed by academic brain trusters, "young, free-wheeling, and discontented," moved steadily to apply the new welfare economics to the management of the entire economy. Public works projects to provide work for the unemployed, stabilization of prices, sound money, a sound banking system, and control over securities sales were only a few of the New Deal measures. Workers were helped to organize, first through Section 7a of the NRA, and later, when the Supreme Court declared the NRA to be unconstitutional, by the Wagner Act.

Step by step, the laws of the land were fitted to the new principles. Dean Roscoe Pound, in his *Spirit of the Common Law,* described how the common law had evolved from its primary purpose, the protection of property, into the legal principle of execution of the "public interest."

It was this new principle, freely applied, which furnished the basis for the economic revolution of the New Deal. Economic rewards, so the new philosophy ran, should not be parceled out by any natural law of self-interest or risk taking, but should vary according to the social usefulness of accomplishment. Surplus income should no longer be the exclusive concern of the businessman who produced it, but should be diverted to contribute to the welfare of society. Investment should produce some social benefit; hence, social investment had to increase. This meant that the institutions to promote social improvement had to be enlarged in scope and authority, usually at the expense of private rich institutions.

The Keynesian Rationale

It was a British scholar and public servant who provided the theoretical basis for this system. John Maynard Keynes, economist, Cambridge don, governor of the Bank of England, and a leading member of the intellectual Bloomsbury group, had devised a theory that accounted perfectly for the system that was so pleasing to the American in the street in the thirties. First in his *Treatise on Money*, and later in his abstruse *General Theory of Employment, Interest and Money*, Keynes pointed an accusing finger at savings as the root of the problem. The key to economic good health was income and, most specifically, national income. The trouble with pure capitalism, Keynes declared, was that it could settle down indefinitely at a point where less than full employment existed. When this condition prevailed there was nothing in the system that would automatically cause it to begin its upward movement again because savings wouldn't be invested by expanding business firms without some outside stimulus.

The key, then, was to get the investment flow started again. This could only be done if the whole economy were managed and viewed as a whole. Then, whenever investment sagged in the private sector, it should be bolstered with an infusion of public investment.

Keynes had come to Washington in 1934 to talk with President Roosevelt, and his *General Theory* was published two years later. It provided a fine solution to a number of problems that were then pressing on the New Deal. The WPA and the pump-priming policy now had a theory to back them up. The depression had a new and plausible explanation which didn't require that we turn the nation over to a new Mussolini. Instead, it permitted democratic management of the entire society—including its economics. The only limitations were that the elected managers submit themselves periodically—according to constitutional and traditional patterns—to the mandate of the voters. All this promised the salvation of capitalism in the form of an "administered capitalism" in which the benefits of large-scale production and private property could be wedded to those of welfare economics.

As it happened, this was also a propitious time for the New Deal to find such an erudite and satisfactory theory to explain what it had been doing, and intended to continue doing. The business community, through the National Association of Manufacturers, the U.S. Chamber of Commerce, and other employer groups, had begun to clamor for a return to the "free private enterprise" system which, they declared, had now righted itself and was back on the track once more. Commuter trains from Westchester, Morristown, and Long Island buzzed with bitterly personal jokes and barbed comments on "that man." Business pressed its case through the Republican party, with organized "Hate Roosevelt" vigor that extended to his wife, his sons, and his dog. Yet, armed with sagacious politics and the new theory, the Democratic party swept over a hapless Alf Landon in 1936, and continued to consolidate its new system. The proponents of risk-taking were kept on the defensive.

Keynes' prophecy that employment and production would respond to controls exerted over savings and investment worked beautifully. Professor Simon Kuznets and his National Bureau of Economic Research worked out a statistical system of national accounts that was so useful that the United States Department of Commerce adopted it in toto and began issuing statements of national income, Gross National Product, personal disposable income, and similar aggregative measures of economic health.

Despite the protests of the various employer groups, the operating executives of leading corporations found that these barometers of economic health were actually invaluable in making business decisions and reducing the uninsurable risks of running a business. Marketing analysts treated the data with respect and applied them with great ingenuity. Thus one large soap company began regularly measuring its annual sales as a "percentage of personal disposable income," increasing advertising when it failed to get its share of what the Commerce Department statisticians reported to be the total size of the cake to be sliced. As war approached, the national income accounts became a vital instrument in the strategy of managing the economy.

The unhappy murmurs of the nation's top executives over the decline of capitalism continued, but in the middle-management ranks there emerged a new crop of young men—the market researchers, accountants, sales managers, production managers, and personnel men whose jobs seemed more secure if risk were reduced —and the centralized manipulations of the economy were continued. The tax rate which bit so excruciatingly into profit after a decade became a familiar hair shirt around which the corporate administrator geared his plans. Then, in 1946, the extraordinary taxation of wartime was eased, profits leaped, companies grew and prospered, and private business found less and less reason to protest.

If the disconsolate business community in 1930 and 1931 saw hope only in a new Mussolini, Roosevelt himself never went this far. From the beginning he declared that his changes were intended to save capitalism by altering its operations rather than eliminating the system itself. In a sense, Roosevelt was more conservative than his critics of the late Thirties, for in his policies he constantly justified big government as a means of conserving our traditions and restoring a more fundamental kind of competition:

> Unhappy events abroad have taught us two simple truths about the liberty of a democratic people.
> The first truth is that the liberty of a democracy is not safe if the people tolerate the growth of private power to a point that it becomes stronger than their democratic state itself. . . .
> The second truth is that the liberty of a democracy is not safe if its business system does not provide employment and produce and distribute goods in such a way as to sustain an acceptable standard of living.

While his critics accused him of actions that would lead to socialism, Roosevelt's rationale was that he was defending capitalism by making it possible for it to survive. Above all he laid upon the economic system the supra-economic goals of democracy and the welfare of individuals, to be achieved through government control over the private collectivisms which distorted the workings of economic-political democracy.

The Challenge of the Peace

In 1945 a crucial shift in direction took place. With the end of the war approaching, the New Deal liberals looked forward to a postwar recession, which they proposed to meet with even more ambitious plans for extension of the managed economy. Hans Christian Sonne, Stuart Chase, and Beardsley Ruml in America, and Lord Woolton in England all came up with plans for coping with the peacetime recession that would follow the defeat of Germany. These pundits seem to have overlooked the fact that though business had produced a mere $100 millions worth of consumer goods in 1944, it had also produced another $90 billions for the war. Private planning, the pent-up demand for consumer goods, the high level of private savings, and certain developments that had been perfected in expanded wartime research, combined to bring about increasing business activity and rising employment. As one Democratic politician put it, "The trouble is, we ran out of poor people." Thus the planned economy, based on the assumption that the gloomy characteristics of 1932 would recur, never appeared. Its place was taken by private corporate planning for the peace.

In 1945 Senator Murray introduced for discussion a Full Employment Act, which in 1946 made full employment a matter of public policy. This law created a Council of Economic Advisors to the President, and a joint committee that would keep the situation under surveillance. Henceforth, the President was to issue an annual economic report to the nation. This report, closely geared to the budget recommendations for the following year, became the principal barometer of the administered economy—risk was to be tamed at last.

The voice of the old "free enterpriser," harking back to the days of the glorious twenties, grew fainter. In the Senate, Robert Taft, Bourke Hickenlooper, Karl Mundt, Charles Halleck, and Everett Dirksen dominated the Republican party, and with each passing year became less effective. Inside business, the key positions in the corporate bureaucracies went increasingly to the middle managers who had been trained academically in Keynesian economics and unreservedly accepted the modern world of strong government and a riskless economy. The dwindling numbers of free enterprisers at the top decried the loss of incentive and freedom implicit in everything the Truman administration did. Both the organization man— or the committee—was making more and more decisions, all aimed at the eradication of risk. In 1952 the election of Dwight D. Eisenhower tamped the turf solidly over the last hopes of the free enterprisers who were looking for one more chance to try nineteenth-century capitalism in America.

The Conservative Reformers

In every presidential election from 1932 to 1952, the traditional Republican pattern of orthodoxy in social matters, conservatism in economics, states rights, nationalism, and, for the most part, high tariffs, had dominated the GOP's platform. A shift in foreign policy away from nationalism took place in 1940, when Willkie and Vandenburg were the front runners. But every time a presidential election drew near, the powerful conservatives—the industrialists, bankers, and corporation lawyers, scions of an older day—threw their financial weight behind the Taft-Dirksen segment of the party. Almost invariably, the Republican platform took its stand on a "return to the basic values of the past." Time and again, this appeal failed.

In July 1952, a profound change took place. The GOP convention shunted aside both Thomas E. Dewey, who had missed the presidency by a hair in 1948, and "Mr. Republican" himself, Robert A. Taft, in favor of a national hero, Dwight D. Eisenhower. Though the general's political convictions were practically unknown, he drew the support of a new liberal wing of the party and was nominated on the first ballot.

The young men who backed the World War II hero wanted a man who could rise above nationalism and lead the United States in a realistic foreign policy. With the war in Korea still dragging on, they felt the need for military leadership as well. But most importantly, they sought a man who could put the brake on a too-rapid expansion of the high-tax, welfare state the Democrats had built. At the same time, they had no desire to reverse the popular reforms of the New Deal. The need of the party was for a man who could convince the worker and the farmer that he was the candidate to vote for, aside from being at the same time obviously someone in whom businessmen could place their confidence also. As no candidate of either party had been able to do in recent years, Eisenhower succeeded in casting a universal spell over the voters.

THE ORGANIZATION MAN'S PRESIDENT

The phenomenon of a conservative leader unseating liberals, only to adopt and prudently extend the most popular reforms they had battled to win, was not unparalleled in the Western world. Disraeli had done the same in nineteenth-century England. With his "New Republicanism," Eisenhower proceeded by degrees to enlarge and consolidate the reforms of the New Deal. This he did with the approval of the corporate organization men and the population at large. It was only the Republicans of the right who saw with dismay his administration moving "counter to the traditional principles of the party."

The likelihood of serious opposition was reduced by the death of Senator Taft, whose passing left a void that was only in small part filled later by Senator Barry Goldwater. The conservative wing of the party could muster no one of Taft's intellectual or moral stature. So Eisenhower, his cabinet staffed with corporation executives and Wall Street lawyers, was able to proceed along a path that his conservative and liberal critics alike dubbed "me-too-ism."

Thus from 1952 to 1960 the managed, riskless capitalism born of the New Deal continued to grow under a Republican administration, this time with the active and energetic support of the business community itself. The Department of Health, Education and Welfare was established as an agency of Cabinet rank, thus formalizing an annual expenditure of four billion dollars on social welfare. In 1958 the Small Business Administration, whose purpose was to reduce risk for small firms that couldn't compete, became a permanent government agency. Government policy turned toward manipulation of the entire economy with the aim of eradicating a new evil—inflation.

For eight years Eisenhower's "conservative" administration

operated on supra-Keynesian economic policies with the enthusiastic—if gradually diminishing—assistance of business. The entire
pattern left the liberal "baffled, impotent, and irrelevant" as continued prosperity, coupled with occasionally infuriating conservative
controls, such as the Landrum-Griffin Act, were accompanied by un-
balanced budgets and vigorous antitrust enforcement. Keynes himself would have been astonished by the uses to which his general
theory was being put by the government of administered capitalism.
Instead of cyclical budgets showing surpluses in good times and
deficits in lean ones, the new pattern was one of constant deficit,
with two accidental exceptions. The new goals of administered
capitalism shifted from the prevention of unemployment to the
continuation of economic growth—as measured by the Gross National Product—without undue inflation.

The updated Keynesian economics, which the now-deceased
Briton would not have recognized, had been described by Truman's
economic advisor, Leon Keyserling, as resembling the application of
the "break-even chart" to national accounts. If we continued to
expand, even if we did so by controlled inflation—so the theory
went—then the size of the national debt accrued in past years
would become insignificant. Indeed, the public expenditures of 1939
looked like a bargain since they were made in dollars that were
being repaid with 1955 dollars now worth only 50 cents. Not only
that, but a fixed rate of taxation, say 20% of Gross National Product,
would produce $100 billion in 1960 whereas, ten years earlier, the
same rate would have produced only $52 billion. Thus, the gains of
economic health could now be obtained without risk to anyone.

In many respects, the cooperation between big government and
big business was a felicitous arrangement. Certainly, the high rate
of government expenditure necessitated profitable businesses, since
it was from profits that most taxes came. It was not surprising that
Maurice Stans, Eisenhower's Budget Director, showed as much concern for corporate profits as did stockholders—perhaps even more.

In expanding markets for new products, there was no stauncher
proponent of the principle that savings were economically undesirable than the corporate vice president of marketing. Everyone
bought on credit, a system that created a whole generation of young

married people whose principal concern was, "how much are the weekly payments?"

Management Without Risk

In every staff department, corporate experts accepted and learned to live with the Keynesian system. The influx of businessmen into government positions, and the flow of former cabinet officers and top military brass into corporate headquarters eased some of the misunderstanding between the two groups. In many respects it became difficult to determine where private government left off and public government began. At the management development courses that began to proliferate during the Fifties, it was found that government administrators and business executives could together study management principles and find no basic areas of disagreement. The installation of "performance budgets" in government agencies bred a growing number of civil servants who were called upon to meet "revolving fund" budgets, which meant mainly that they had to recoup all costs, operate efficiently, and please their customers. In private business, risk-taking without fear of depression became mere administrative practice.

The Not-So-New Frontier of the Sixties

Because Eisenhower's policies resembled Roosevelt's and Truman's, his opponent could find little to attack. The outsiders twitted the administration over the President's preoccupation with golf and his inept handling of press conferences, but could make no significant criticisms of what the government was doing. To the general public, including businessmen, workers, housewives and professionals, things seemed to be working well. If there was any dissatisfaction at all, it tended to be more in the nature of vague uneasiness over leadership style than in its results. Only the intellectuals were apparently totally dissatisfied, and wrote devastating criticisms about the hollowness of our "affluent society."

Adlai Stevenson, darling of the intellectuals, captured the Democratic nomination in 1956. Once more he was overwhelmed by the Eisenhower juggernaut, and with that defeat went his chance to run against Nixon in 1960.

It was his total mastery of the political situation that brought John F. Kennedy to office, uniting the intellectuals and—by a minuscule margin—the people at large behind him. But the high hopes of the New Deal liberals for a resurgence of accelerated centralized control failed to materialize during the Kennedy administration. After three years, the only apparent difference between him and his predecessor was his personalized style of leadership of the same old instruments of administered capitalism.

To the middle manager, Kennedy proved an appealing leader. In one of his few attempts to apply his personal form of "vigorous management" to the economy—the steel price controversy of 1962— he was chastened by the spate of "Hate Kennedy" jokes it evoked, and immediately offered tax cuts and depreciation write-offs to placate the business community. Meanwhile, his cabinet included corporation executives, bankers, and Wall Street lawyers in generous supply. Rather than Walter Reuther's obtaining a private key to the side door of the White House, as jubilant liberals had hoped for, it was the president of the giant Ford Motor Company on whom that privilege was bestowed.

Whatever influence the ultra-conservatives may have had over college students and a few corporate chief executives who were still living in the past, they completely failed to mobilize the great corps of middle managers or the general public. Concerned primarily with the problems of quality control, market planning, product development, and personnel administration, the bureaucrat in the corporation began to look more and more like the bureaucrat in government. The two were alike, also, in their essentially apolitical nature. Periodic attempts to spur business managers into taking an active interest in government and politics through courses in "public affairs" and political action made little real impact on this entrenched indifference.

In 1964, Lyndon B. Johnson pulled surprisingly well for a Democratic candidate among corporation officers and middle managers. Traditionally Republican, they found it easier to identify with a candidate who looked comfortably businesslike, and said few, if any, alarming things which might require the voter to think ideologically. An amazing touch with business was established by Johnson's cost reduction programs, turning out lights in the White House, and heartily supporting the Secretary of Defense who promised— and delivered—efficiency and businesslike practices in the mammoth Department of Defense. If he talked of the "Great Society" at the height of the campaign, there was little here to alarm the new capitalist. After all, a fellow who would cut taxes on business couldn't be wholly bad. Meticulously avoiding direct attacks on business (or anyone else except his opponent), Johnson made the future of business capitalism, strongly influenced by Washington, seem somehow less foreboding.

Recent surveys have shown today's manager as ranging from tolerant to casually approving of many of the specific instruments of administered capitalism. Surrounded by the accoutrements of security and stability, he has become increasingly preoccupied with the devices of administration. After a decent tour in some specialist capacity he focuses his attention on mastering the skills of organization, planning, controlling, coordinating, and human relations. As his concern for the risk-gain calculus diminishes, he becomes more and more the master of administration as an end in itself. He has learned that administrative ability is transferable not only from one department to another, but from one company to the next.

Leaders and Administrators

A major consequence of this trend has been the increasing division between those who *administer* and those who genuinely *manage*. The administrator is a man who adapts to his environment in order to survive in and obtain sustenance from it. The risk-oriented manager relates to his environment—including the people in it—in order to control it, to manipulate it, and to direct it for gain.

The sad fact is that the world of administered capitalism has bred a surplus of administrators and a crucial shortage of managers. The gloomy prophecy of Schumpeter quoted at the head of this chapter has been fulfilled in the corporate, division, and plant offices of leading companies all over America. The result has been to facilitate the next stage in the decline of capitalism.

Thanks to the well-accepted and adroitly applied "snubbers" that have been built into administered capitalism, the chances of reinstating the once-potent identification of liberalism with the exploited, the unfortunate, and the oppressed are now negligible. Consequently, a new form of liberalism has emerged which draws its strength from the discontent found in simple boredom and conformity.

The Quest for a Larger Meaning to Business

Not long ago, a well-known plumbing contractor died in a midwestern city. Compared with that of the atomic physicist, the Arctic explorer, or the novelist, his was hardly a glorious occupation. Yet his passing brought sadness to an unusual number of persons from all walks of life. As the young priest who presided over the last rites noted:

> Throughout his entire life, this man devoted himself to making his immediate world a more healthy place in which to live. His zeal for better standards in his field may well have prolonged many lives. Through his example, the younger men who have now taken his place in his business have acquired a zeal for high health standards and excellence that will serve this community well. Magnanimous toward other men, quick to lash out against shoddy work wherever he saw it, firm in his convictions, this man was representative of business at its best.

A trivial illustration? Possibly.

Yet surely this man met all the standards of what a business man could be from the viewpoint of society. He raised the standard of living of his community. He took chances. His zeal for excellence served him well, and he prospered. He was honorable in his dealings with others and could hold his head high.

The point of all this is that in any business there is an opportunity for service and human betterment that can best be realized by being a good businessman first. Imbuing businessmen with this idea may be more important than schooling them in the skills, tools, and principles of scientific management or in capitalist dogma. If corporate size stamps out the opportunity for each man to make a simple contribution to society through zeal for achieving his own business goals, coupled with some small moral fervor, then Schumpeter's march to socialism will strike many as a welcome journey.

Administrators—Public and Private

Since we have already reached the stage where the behavior of the professional administrator in business is almost indistinguishable from that of the professional administrator in government, it hardly seems likely that any great wellspring of resistance to further socialization of the economy is being generated. Presidents of automobile companies can move in and out of cabinet positions and find that they have similar subordinates to direct in either situation. It's not inconceivable, then, that there should be a massive indifference among middle and lower managers to whether the remote chief at the top of the hierarchy is appointed by a self-perpetuating board of directors or by a central planning board in Washington. In fact, in the event of crisis in which their place in the bureaucratic structure were threatened, they might actually welcome the latter arrangement, if it protected their status and reduced their anxiety.

Is there nothing, then, to distinguish corporate management from government administration? Only personal risk! Yet one graduate school trains students of business and students of public administration side by side—simply as employees in bureaucracies.

Alfred North Whitehead once said that a great society is one in which men of business think greatly about their function. What does this great thinking consist of for the vast corps of corporate middle managers?

Perhaps Schumpeter's gloomy prediction could be averted if some distinguishing personalized business goals could be put before the growing army of corporate bureaucrats. Perhaps we might paraphrase Whitehead, calling on our plumbing contractor as an example, and suggest: "A great society is one in which little men think greatly about their small functions." A system of managing which encourages such behavior is badly needed. *Managers without personal commitment to risk and the possibility of personal failure are bureaucrats.*

CHAPTER 3

The Decline of
Risk Bearing

Slowly—or perhaps not so slowly—industrial United States is moving toward a form of economic republic without historical precedent.

—ADOLPH A. BERLE

Joseph Schumpeter had a mind that constantly dismayed those who most would have liked to be found in agreement with him. Like the late Senator Robert Taft in the related field of politics, he often straddled issues in seemingly paradoxical fashion. In one breath he asked, "Can capitalism survive? No, I don't think it can." And in the next he demolished the critics of capitalism in the most ultra-conservative manner. An admirer of Marx as a theorist, he also held that "in capitalism somebody must get hurt," and proposed that occasional unemployment was a cheap price to pay for the gains which it brought in economic growth.

Schumpeter saw his "march into socialism" as a migration of the people's economic power from the private into the public sphere and cited four major trends in the recent economic history of the United States as the reasons for believing that this march would not halt.

In the first place, the very success of business in creating a new high standard of living for society bred its ultimate control by political forces through its own bureaucratization.

Secondly, the "rational" nature of capitalism spreads rational habits of mind, and free contracts between superior and subordinate tend to destroy a system based solely upon everyone seeking his own short-run utilitarian ends.

Furthermore, because business men concentrated on the technology of managing plants and offices, there sprang into being a political system and intellectual class independent of, and hostile to, the interests of corporate business.

And, finally, the value system of capitalism has bred counter values of security, equality, and regulation which must ultimately overwhelm it.

The civilization of inequality and the family fortune were—so Schumpeter declared—basic to the capitalistic system. Capitalism might still provide economic growth, however, so long as capitalists behaved like capitalists. That is, so long as they showed the innovative temperament, the daring, and the spirited willingness to stake their personal fortunes on the chance of great gains through new ideas, breakthroughs, and innovation. Such people, Schumpeter suggested, have become rarer and rarer as capitalism itself has created corps of administrators, pale, gray-clad, and gray-spirited men who listen too closely to the intellectuals who surround them and to the dictates of their own fears—all this in an environment that their predecessors daringly created.

Productivity and Innovation

With the same voice as he predicted socialism Schumpeter also defended capitalism. His theme was no simple, soothing, apologia for the system of the consumer vote, but a more unflinching—occasionally even truculent—defense of pure capitalism, capitalism the supreme producer. Citing the growth of production through good times and bad for sixty years prior to 1928, he noted that, measured in real terms, the distribution of this constant gain of production of two per cent per year had substantially changed in favor of the low-income groups:

This follows from the fact that the capitalist engine is first and last an engine of mass production, which unavoidably means also production for the masses.

Schumpeter then went on to explode the idea that the rich get richer and the poor get poorer under capitalism. Noting that the higher-income groups spend more of their money for services, he pointed out that it is the cheap cloth, boots, and motor cars that are the typical achievements of capitalism, and not, as a rule, the kind of improvements that would mean much to a rich man. "The capitalist achievement," Schumpeter declared, "does not consist in providing silk stockings for queens but in bringing them within the reach of factory girls in return for steadily decreasing amounts of effort."

The risks in the process, he went on, are tied to the gains, and can be summarized in two aspects of capitalism: the business cycle and attendant unemployment. Unemployment, he frankly conceded, was "among those evils which, like poverty, capitalist evolution could never eliminate of itself."

A second risk is the personal prosperity of the risk-taker; formerly the owner, today the manager. But in eradicating the former, we've erased the latter.

How, then, should we cope with such evils?

For one thing, it's evident that the rate of unemployment for the 60 years prior to World War I showed a horizontal trend. Bad as this may have been, it was an inescapable condition of capitalism, but not one that feeds on itself and worsens. Moreover, it was counterbalanced by the constantly increasing production that accompanied capitalism. If the system had had another run like the sixty years before World War I, it would have met all the desiderata of the social reformers—including most of the cranks—without any interference with the capitalist process. From such a rising production and its increasing tendency to distribute its output widely among the lower-income groups, "ample provision for the unemployed, in particular, would then be not only a tolerable but a light burden."

But from the viewpoint of its implications for managerial style, Schumpeter's theory of business cycles is more pertinent than his defense of capitalism. The theory of cycles centers on the businessman, the "entrepreneur" himself as the initiator of action that disturbs economic equilibrium and ultimately raises productive levels. It is the risk-taking manager in quest of profits or personal prosperity who makes innovations in business. Expansion doesn't come about simply through stealing customers from others, or playing what modern game theorists would call a "zero-sum, two-person game" in a specific market. The entrepreneur invents and innovates, then persuades bankers to extend him credit, bidding up interest rates and paying higher wages to induce labor into his vacant positions. Wages and prices rise. This has a weakening effect on profits, and a general period of inactivity and falling-off in innovation occurs. The expansion period of the cycle depends upon the time required for the invention to be introduced into the economic system through the installation of new processes and equipment. Thus it is that, through innovation and disruption of the status quo, originating with risk-minded business leaders, the capitalistic system expands, economic growth occurs, and capitalism, the producer, raises the standard of living for all.

At the heart of Schumpeter's theory is the innovator, the tradition breaker, the disrupter of the status quo in the garb of a bourgeois economic prince. His own dissatisfaction with things as they are, coupled with his personal initiative in introducing change underlies all economic growth, and also accounts for periodic slumps. The two, Schumpeter implied, are related, and one is the price that must be paid for the other. Economic growth demands innovation, and innovation requires compelling business leadership to make it happen. The hope of gain lies in the prospect of increased productivity, so that interest can be earned. The alternative, Schumpeter suggested, is a state of equilibrium in which saving and investment in the past are balanced by the consumption of the present.

Furthermore, Schumpeter argued, capitalism attracts the best brains to business. Spectacular prizes bring forth men of "ability and energy and supernormal capacity for work" far more than an equal distribution of rewards would do. Such individual risk-taking leaders are selected not by management development programs or performance appraisal forms, but by the system itself to which individuals are chained by the bourgeois value systems that accompany capitalism. Thus obsolete methods and incompetent men are swept away. Failure also threatens the able man, thus whipping the leadership into more productive effort than a more just system of penalties or a more logical system of selection could ever do.

The Taming of Risk

Despite his strenuous arguments for the capitalist system, Schumpeter predicted its decline on the grounds of the decline of risk-taking and the dwindling possibility of spectacular gain. The very fruits of productivity that capitalism generated had bred a social system that was obstructive to the entrepreneur. Where Marx had envisioned the end of capitalism in violent capture of the machinery of production by the masses, Schumpeter saw its demise implicit in "administered capitalism." In socialist eyes, corporate enterprise is an economic system that will not function except on capitalist lines. No alternative exists for the central planner but to run it according to its own logic, but in the interests of its proletarian constituency. Public and private collectivism and bureaucracy are the result.

Even while Schumpeter was writing, evidence was accumulating that bore out his case. Adolph Berle and Gardiner Means focused the microscope of economic research on the growth of corporations as dominant social institutions and concluded, "Corporations have ceased to be merely legal devices through which the private business transactions of individuals may be carried on." The corporation, owning the dominant share of productive property in society, though its owners comprised only a minuscule fraction of the population, was both a method of property tenure and a means of organizing economic life. The end effect of this increasing size would be the disappearance of private enterprise. In fact, Berle and Means concluded, the corporate enterprise was taking on the dimensions of a system just as feudalism had been a system. Moreover, they noted:

> Only to the extent that any worker seeks advancement within an organization is there room for initiative—an initiative that can be exercised within the narrow range of function he is called upon to perform.

Here was clearly a denial that capitalism, as Adam Smith had described it, even existed any more. Under his classical schema, the motive for production was conceived to be self-interest, "but the guidance of this motive, so that it conduces to the interest of all concerned, is brought about by the mechanism of the market and the force of competition." This whole concept was now considered dead.

Eight years after Schumpeter's book appeared, prominent businessmen were calling for a better description than Adam Smith's of modern corporate capitalism, on the ground that classical economics had "lost touch with the colossal developments of the last forty years." Businessman Oswald Knauth calmly declared that in meeting the exigencies of the modern world, businessmen had fashioned a new form of economy.

How had this affected the role of the risk-bearer and rambunctious destroyer of the status quo? According to Knauth, a major effect was the rise of *impersonal* leadership. "Decisions are made by groups and not by individuals." Only the chief executive can express his personality, said Knauth, "and he does so by putting his imprint on the system rather than determining particular policies." Employees, presumably including the leaders in the corporate system, surrendered their personal liberty voluntarily, and the hero or superman of the capitalist society was extinct.

The upshot was the rise of managerial enterprise, a new system which supplanted risk and tamed it, but lacked a clear definition of its own nature, and had no codes or natural forces to guide it. Essentially, it was defenseless against the charges of recklessness and irresponsibility that had been accepted as part and parcel of capitalist risk-taking.

In a sense, though, there was perhaps one code by which the new system could abide. By common agreement the impact of any individual was held to be insignificant. But this seemed to be the limit of the system's logic. Beyond this, it was surrounded by an ice cap of managerial skills, tools and philosophies centered in group decision making and on the eradication of the zest, innovation, and change that are rooted in the hope of great personal gain.

Today every large corporation has its department of stockholder relations, testifying to the need to insulate chief executives from pressures that might stimulate excessive interest in larger gains at risk to the owners. The major airlines assist one another by sharing profits during a national strike, thus eliminating the risk emanating from strong collective bargaining.

Among the fastest-growing industries these days are those financial and banking institutions that sell what John R. Commons called risk-prevention services, assuring bureaucrats of the eradication of actuarially determinable hazards. The areas of uninsurable risks in business are constantly being reduced, and for sound economic reasons. The administrator is a preserver rather than an innovator.

Inside the corporation, there has been a marked proliferation of risk-reduction departments. Armed with the tools of modern mathematics, they have introduced a more rational concept of risk than was heretofore possible. By devising predictive models rooted in empirical studies of the past, management hence now produces self-fulfilling prophecies of risk management in the future. The true significance of these developments lies less in their rationality than in their general proposition that risk itself can be removed from the area of uncertainty, and turned into statistical and mathematical certainty.

The Creative-Destructive Hypothesis

Though there was some similarity between the views of Berle and Means and those of Schumpeter, there were also sharp differences. The Berle and Means studies of concentration in industry led them to the conclusion that competition was dead. Schumpeter scoffed at this idea, holding that mutations in the form of capitalism were necessary, but this did not mean that competition was extinct, or that the corporation was no longer subject to the mechanism of the market. The new capitalism of the corporate society was an evolutionary phase from which capitalism could emerge stronger and more socially useful than before. This would be achieved by a process of *creative destruction*, Schumpeter said, because capitalism is "by nature a form of method of economic change" and not only "never was but never can be stationary."

Competition emerging from pure price bases naturally evolved through this process into monopolistic competition, whose *modus operandi* was to discipline before it attacked. The large-scale production required to achieve economies does not call for despair over the system, but understanding. On the record, Schumpeter stoutly insisted, monopolistic competition or oligopoly led in the long run not to price increases, but exactly the reverse. The steady increase in output through innovation and the creative destruction of existing businesses by better ones was so prevalent in modern corporate society that if large firms attempted to fix extortionate prices (as most would do according to classical theory), they would find the ground slipping from beneath their feet. No company becomes so large or so secure in its market position that it can ignore the possibility of another introducing change through innovation and wiping it out. In the large corporate entity, survival, then, was as real a problem as of old, requiring as much attention to innovation and vitality as it ever had done.

Schumpeter's stand was not without its critics, however. Polanyi, pointing to the great transformation that had overtaken us, concluded "nineteenth-century civilization has collapsed." Stretching his horizons beyond pure economics, he surmised that this collapse had come about through the failure of the balance-of-power system, the international gold standard, the liberal state, and the self-regulatory market. It was the latter which drew his sharpest fire. Polanyi further declared that the main failure of capitalism had been in its inability to understand the problem of change. The self-adjusting market was "stark utopia," which couldn't exist for any length of time without "annihilating the human and natural substance of society." Had it continued, in the end it would have physically destroyed men and "transformed its surroundings into a wilderness." Hence Polanyi denounced what he termed "a mystical readiness to accept the social consequences of economic improvements, whatever they might be."

Bureaucratic Leadership

Obviously the preservation of the new capitalism in its mutated form called for different styles of leadership from those that had characterized the actions of the old merchant prince or the early capitalist manufacturer. To make creative destruction work forcibly for the preservation of capitalism, innovation and the sweeping away of less effective enterprises had to be rampant. But the successful execution of this most necessary process was blocked by the internal forces of self-generated bureaucracy.

The vast wastelands of passive and dependent people in middle-management positions, the concept of the administrator as the person who by situation and temperament *prevents* things from happening, bore within them the seeds of capitalism's downfall. Far more deleterious than the ranting of radicals, or the conspiracies of bomb-throwing Marxists, were the blockers on the corporate payroll, the security-minded managers.

The reduction of administration to a science was undoubtedly another contributing factor. In such an environment, the natural innovator or the visionary found himself up against a value system in which there was no more nervous form of behavior than "rocking the boat."

While the new industrial society went beyond the capitalism of classical economics, it failed to follow the path predicted by Marx who envisioned capitalist competition leading to gluts of commodities that would bring about business crises in which small firms would go under and the large firms grow larger. This, Marx said, would lead, in turn, to an increase in the number of working-class people, whose misery would grow with their enlarging numbers. Thus the rich would get richer and the poor would get poorer, and the inevitable end would be crises in which the masses would finally take over. The spectacular failure of this prediction does not mean, however, that the new industrial society does not have some hefty problems of its own.

The major blocks to the creation of a society of high production and rising standards of living lie not so much in our institutional forms and economic organization as in the suppression of risk taking which the industrial society has built into its very fiber. Concern over equitable distribution and the alleviation of discontent growing out of people's ego and social needs have diverted our attention from the fact that our physical needs can be satisfied. They will remain so if we retain the basically productive orientation of our system. Over-attention to equitable distribution of the existing product can only have the inevitable effect of proliferating bureaucracy inside business, blunting its growth, and stemming innovation.

One end-effect of bureaucratic leadership is the decline of innovation. If there is one thing an administrator in a bureaucracy cannot abide it is chance taking or individuals being held accountable for results. His value system revolves around the preservation of the status quo, especially his own. In his eyes, the triple goals of organization, planning, and control, which comprise the bulk of most executive development courses, are perfectly suitable and practical methods of achieving this objective. Administrative practices and human relations, as he studiously pursues them, have pertinence as they insure bureaucratic proliferation of administrators and self-maintenance, at the expense of growth if necessary.

The New Authority

Life in the crystal palaces of corporate headquarters is considered normal and satisfactory when it is *quiet*. The placid and secure pace of men without anxiety pervades the ranks of the middle-management body politic. Since risks are widely shared, it is the "system" that bears the brunt of bringing on innovation. Errors are fewer, since the possibilities of large gains, involving as they must the risk of larger losses, are eschewed. The hierarchy exerts its group authority from above to minimize the individual authority of those below. Committees occupy three-quarters of the typical executive's time, according to one study. Touching bases on a field with ten bases keeps functionaries padding quietly over headquarters rugs the whole of their working lives.

In fact, the new leader makes no decisions, but operates a decision-making apparatus, reports Professor Mason Haire of the University of California. And Professor Douglas McGregor, of the Massachusetts Institute of Technology, says that leadership is a relationship, rather than a function performed by one man, pulling together a symbolic chief and participating followers. Three forces work to shape the actions of leaders in the new corporate society: (1) *Selection* for the qualities which make for effective membership in the bureaucratic framework, (2) *training* in scientific management and rational systems of leadership and executive functioning, and (3) *alteration of the environment,* to isolate and possibly expel the traditional entrepreneur and risk-taker and the innovator from any sensitive location where his impact might be disruptive.

Even the small businessman models himself on this new style of corporate leadership. Having inherited the business, he graduates from Harvard, buys a pin-striped suit, a pair of half-glasses, Danish furniture for his office, and joins with other members of the Young President's Organization in taking sensitivity training. Regular checks from the Small Business Administration ease hard times in the market.

Schumpeter's prediction, made some fifteen years ago, would then appear to have some pertinence today. Does the decline of capitalism, and the new style of business leadership point inevitably, then, to socialism? Not necessarily. Things happen because people want them to happen. The restoration of innovation and vision in leadership isn't impossible, even in the noncapitalistic, yet still non-socialist, corporate system we live in. That restoration won't come automatically, however. It can only happen if managers make it happen.

Though we may agree that Schumpeter was right in predicting the demise of old-style capitalism, this doesn't necessarily point to the conclusion that socialism is the only remedy for a society in revulsion against the oppressive effects of the old system. The belief that a society must be either "right" or "left" was actually the product of a world accustomed to thinking in ideological terms.

The modern world, however, is in no mood to think in this way. Gladstone might have blushed to be caught unaware of the latest political theory; but since 1918, statesmen of all political hues have tended to dislike the academic and ideological theorist. As a result, says Professor Isaiah Berlin, no "commanding work of political philosophy has appeared in the twentieth century." Though his critics have refuted this conclusion by pointing to the works of Lenin and Mao Tse-tung, they agree that there is no philosophy of freedom uniting the Western world. Schumpeter belonged to an earlier generation, and thus thought in ideological terms. Modern man adheres more to the position that ideology is the "opium of the intellectuals" and deals with his problems as they come.

In fact, to use the word "socialism" to describe our coming condition is now mere gong-striking. The sound reverberates, but there is no longer any substance to it. It is more to the point to recognize that our environment now dictates the adoption of a more compelling kind of business leadership—the kind of leadership that will restore to the individual manager his personal risk for loss or gain.

In the following chapters we shall show how the system of management by objectives incorporates most of the requirements for this kind of leadership.

CHAPTER 4

The System of
Management By Objectives

*The systems concept is primarily a way
of thinking about the job of managing.*
—R. Johnson, F. A. Kast, and J. E. Rosensweig

At the outset, let's make it plain that the
system of management by objectives goes beyond being a set of
rules, a series of procedures, or even a set method of managing. As
the above quotation points out, it is a particular way of thinking
about management. Let's begin, then, by placing our system in its
conceptual framework:

1. The basic structure of the corporation is the organizational
form often called a *hierarchy*. This is the familiar arrangement of
boxes showing the boss in the top box, with two, three, or more
subordinates in the boxes one level down. Management by objectives is a system for making that structure work, and to bring about
more vitality and personal involvement of the people in the hierarchy.

2. Management by objectives provides for the maintenance and
orderly growth of the organization by means of statements of what
is expected for everyone involved, and measurement of what is
actually achieved. It assigns risks to all responsible leaders and
makes their progress—even their tenure—dependent upon their producing results. It stresses the ability and achievements of leaders
rather than their personality.

3. As a system, management by objectives is especially applicable to professional and managerial employees. It can extend as far down as first-line supervisors, and also cover many staff and technical positions. Though the same basic system (measuring results against standards) is used in managing hourly rated or clerical workers, the methods of setting standards and measuring results are significantly different.

4. Management by objectives helps overcome many of the chronic problems of managing managers and professionals. For example:

a. It provides a means of measuring the true contribution of managerial and professional personnel.

b. By defining the common goals of people and organizations and measuring individual contributions to them, it enhances the possibility of obtaining coordinated effort and teamwork without eliminating personal risk taking.

c. It provides solutions to the key problem of defining the major areas of responsibility for each person in the organization, including joint or shared responsibilities.

d. Its processes are geared to achieving the results desired, both for the organization as a whole and for the individual contributors.

e. It eliminates the need for people to change their personalities, as well as for appraising people on the basis of their personality traits.

f. It provides a means of determining each manager's span of control.

g. It offers an answer to the key question of salary administration—"How should we allocate pay increase from available funds, if we want to pay for results?"

h. It aids in identifying potential for advancement and in finding promotable people.

A Brief Definition

In brief, the system of management by objectives can be described as a process whereby the superior and subordinate managers of an organization jointly identify its common goals, define each individual's major areas of responsibility in terms of the results expected of him, and use these measures as guides for operating the unit and assessing the contribution of each of its members.

The words we shall use in describing this system will be those every manager knows. We'll talk about authority, responsibility, delegation, and so on. We'll refer to such familiar procedures as the performance review, the salary review, cost accounting, and other everyday management terms. The reader will not be called upon to master a new glossary or to grapple with the jargon of social science. Why? Because management by objectives is essentially a system of incorporating into a more logical and effective pattern the things many people are already doing, albeit in a somewhat chaotic fashion, or in a way that obscures personal risk and responsibility.

The primary effects of operating by management by objectives are to be seen in such tangible results as improved profit, more growth, lower costs, and increased revenues. On a more intangible plane, it also makes bureaucracy less tenable by affecting such secondary variables as production, quality, housekeeping, sales volume, staff work, and research effectiveness. Its tertiary effects are visible in such areas as better morale, more promotable people, improved quality of service, and improved delegation of decision making.

Sources of Management Knowledge

One of the most obvious facts about management is that there are effective bosses and ineffective ones. An organization may have an impressive array of experts in engineering, investment, purchasing, accounting, finance, sales, and heaven knows what besides, and still fall dismally short of its objectives. Yet later, the same organization, headed by a different manager (or the same manager using different management methods), will succeed brilliantly. How to achieve this "turning around" of an organization is thus the subject of much discussion.

One conclusion that has been reached on this question is that *managing* is a function or activity that affects total organizational performance far more than any other. In fact, it makes the others effective or ineffective.

Another conclusion is that this managerial function is a set of actions and a kind of behavior that is *distinct from the activities it manages.*

How does a man learn how to manage? By and large, there are three basic sources of management knowledge: imitation, situational thinking, and behavioral science.

IMITATION

Probably the greatest single source of management knowledge is the boss's behavior. Thus, the young man finds he is learning how to manage at the same time as he takes direction from a superior. This would suggest that it is sound career planning to choose good bosses to work for. It also implies that the superior has a responsibility to behave in a way that is worthy of imitation, since this will happen anyway.

The biographies as well as the personal examples of successful men are another often-followed guide. This is sound practice, provided the aspiring manager imitates the things that really made thr m successful—not their idiosyncrasies or irrelevant acts.

More dubious are the organized studies of the "career patterns" of successful managers. Slavish or unsophisticated imitation of such things can lead to over-obsession with certain kinds of educational backgrounds or experience as a basis for selection, and the fruitless search for the "executive personality." It also obscures the fact that successful management behavior is usually "situational," that is to say, related to the environment and the followers, as well as to the leader and his actions or personality. Actually—and mere imitation offers no clues here—*objectives* often explain behavior better than any other contributing factor in a managerial situation, since it is these that provide the main energizing and directive force for managerial action.

SITUATIONAL THINKING

The second way of finding out what makes managers successful is through situational analysis and situational thinking. This means that instead of studying the actions of individual managers, we study the entire situation in which they work. Managers work in a variety of environments, and the particular environment in which they are called upon to function can account for their success or failure as often as their personal actions.

Thus, the values and goals of the organization in which the manager works invariably shape his behavior and are often the underlying reason for his success or failure. The manager relates to the organization and gets his work done in, through, and occasionally around it. A knowledge of its values, the way it operates, its people, and its policies is essential in understanding managerial achievement (or its absence).

Every manager also works in an economic environment. The availability of funds, the procedures for accounting, the level of competition, and hundreds of other economic factors must be considered in explaining managerial success.

Figure 4-1

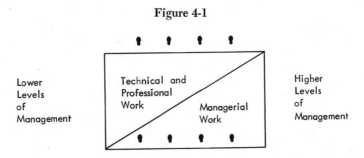

Also to be taken into account is the manager's technical environment. To a considerable extent, the success of managers in such fields as banking, insurance, manufacturing, education, hospital administration, or accounting is shaped by the demands of the profession they manage and practice. Some managers can readily translate from one field to another. A few seem to be able to manage any kind of business. Some can only succeed in a single line.

For the most part, the higher a person goes in the organization, the more time and energy he spends on the managerial portion of his job. For this reason a top military man can move into a top industrial or business post, because at the top, wherever he is, he is exclusively a manager. It is more difficult for a lower-level manager to switch fields, since the technical part of his job will differ from one spot to another.

How the managerial content of a job increases and the technical or professional emphasis decreases as a manager rises in the organization is shown in Figure 4-1.

There are many other situational forces that influence managerial action. Values, custom, mores—all sorts of social and political factors may place special demands on the manager and must be weighed in explaining his behavior.

BEHAVIORAL SCIENCE

Over the past twenty or thirty years, the work of the manager has been the subject of intensive study by behavioral and social scientists. Though these researchers have undoubtedly enlarged our insights into the nature of the manager's job, they do not provide a complete explanation of managerial behavior and effective management action, nor does a knowledge of these findings serve as a substitute for managing.

Figure 4-2

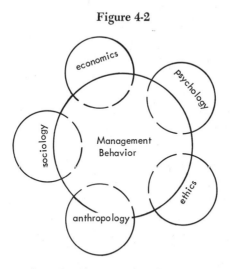

This may perhaps be most graphically seen in Figure 4-2, where the large circle represents the whole range of behavior with which practicing managers are concerned. The surrounding circles are the social and behavioral science disciplines adding to and explaining a part of the manager's functions. *Yet, as the diagram clearly shows, the central core of management knowhow lies in managing, not in the social sciences.*

The manager uses the findings of psychological research to understand, predict, and control such aspects of individual human behavior as learning, motivation, frustration, adjustment, communication, and so on. He uses sociological knowledge to understand how to deal with small groups, cliques, informal organization behavior, crowds, mobs, communities. From the anthropologist, especially the applied cultural anthropologist, he can gain an insight into the problems of cultural patterns in plants and offices. Yet, so far as the average manager is concerned, all these sources of information must be put to work within the relatively simple framework in which most administrative work is done—a formal structure where authority rests near the top and in which goals must be set and results measured.

Most good work in management aims at accomplishing some specific end—achieving a particular goal, solving a particular problem, or reaching some fixed terminal point. The definition of these objectives for the whole organization, for all its subordinate organizations, and for the individuals in them is the logical starting place for management improvement because:

- If you don't have a goal, you have no idea whether you are on the right road or not.
- You can't assess results without some prior expectations against which to measure them.
- You don't know when things are drifting if you aren't clear what goal would comprise "non drifting" or purposive action.
- People can't perform with maximum effectiveness if they don't know what goals the organization is seeking (and why), or how well they are doing in relation to those goals.

The Basic Organization Format

Professor Rensis Likert has described the organization of most firms, universities, and institutions as a series of "linking pins" in which the leader of a lower group is also a member of the next highest group. He illustrates it in Figure 4-3 this way:

Figure 4-3

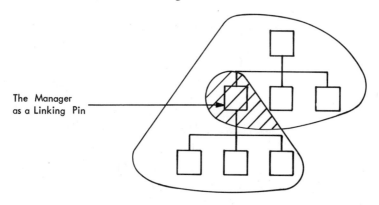

The Manager
as a Linking Pin

Here, we are mainly concerned about those higher-level linking positions, where in fact we are dealing with the "management of managers." At this level, some of the goals will be received from the link above. Others will be developed within the unit.

Let's study that lower link more closely. The major elements in the system are illustrated in Figure 4-4.

1. The manager assumes responsibility for identifying the common goals which all his subordinates share with him, and toward whose achievement he must converge their combined talents.

2. Each person is able to state, in advance of the attempt, *areas of responsibility* and *measures of acceptable results* for his position.

3. Each person has knowledge of the goals he is to achieve, has worked out a plan for achieving them, and is measured by his *results*, insofar as these can be attributed to conditions under his own effective control.

While this system may seem obvious enough, the plain fact is that present systems of managing fall far short of this logical procedure. Michigan psychologist Norman R. F. Maier, in a study that explored the extent to which superiors and subordinates agreed on the major elements of the latter's job, found a divergence of opinion between the two groups on twenty-five per cent of the items.

When a manager is an employee in a large organization, his definition of *success* is inextricably tied to helping his boss succeed. Yet research evidence, in the Maier study and elsewhere, strongly

Figure 4-4

The Basic System Within Which Management Functions

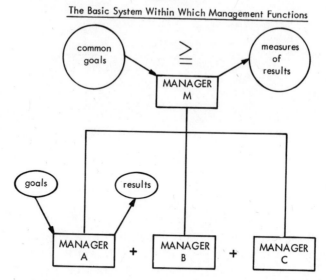

indicates that most subordinate managers aren't really clear about what their boss expects of them. In the absence of such understanding, it's little more than an accident or a special form of clairvoyance when a manager is considered very successful by his boss. The retreat into the security of bureaucratic life naturally ensues.

Let's take a typical organization in which manager M has three supervisors or subordinate managers reporting to him.

Figure 4-5

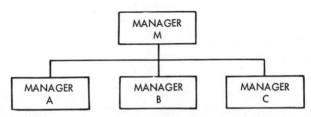

Manager M is concerned about getting maximum effort, creativity, and results from each of his subordinates. He turns his attention to manager A. M constructs a review of A's performance. This view is illustrated in Figure 4-6.

Figure 4-6

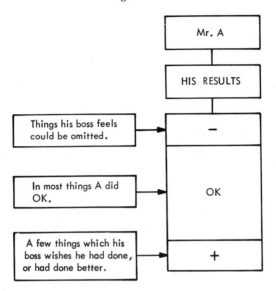

Though in many respects, A's performance was satisfactory, there are some things M wonders why he bothered doing. There are also a few things A failed to do which his boss wishes he had done.

Faced with such a chart of results M turns to the problem of *improving* them for next time. Here he has a choice of the three tools the manager can use to obtain results through the efforts and abilities of others:

1. SELECTION

If he considers A's performance as grossly unsatisfactory, he may select him *out* and thus leave the way open for selecting *in* another man whose results he hopes will be better. If, however, A's good results outweigh those things M is somewhat dissatisfied with, he'll probably not use this tool, but move on to one of the other two available.

2. CONTROL

He may decide that the reason for A's failure to perform to expectations is somehow related to indifference, sloth, laxity, natural distaste for work, or inattention. This, he feels, can be overcome by closer supervision, tighter control, promise of benefit or threat of punishment, pressure, coercion, or some other form of control, and direction. This places a heavier burden upon M to work very hard at overseeing the man more tightly.

3. DEVELOPMENT

Here the manager concludes that lack of knowledge, skill, or ability may account for the results. He starts by imposing controls to discover what A is actually doing or not doing, and imparts this knowledge, skill, or ability at the same time as he gradually relinquishes and eases the controls. When he has eased the controls, if his development efforts have been successful, A will continue under self-control to act satisfactorily on his own.

Using General Motivation Methods As Indirect Controls

If M assumes that the causes of A's failures are sloth, indifference, laxity, or inattention, he may turn to certain popularized kinds of motivational formulae that have been widely disseminated in management and supervisory training courses. As he looks at A's performance for the recent past, he constructs a mental image which resembles Figure 4-7.

Figure 4-7

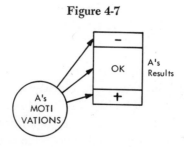

M has learned that men *in toto* are motivated by certain basic needs. These include *physical* needs, *ego* needs, and *social* needs. Thus, his reasoning goes, if he can supply one or more of these in the right combination he can control A's behavior, and, without being a tyrant or an autocrat, can manipulate him into doing the things which he, M, wants done and eliminate the slothful, lacka-daisical or indifferent behavior in those areas where A's performance didn't quite measure up.

M applies these formulae in a variety of specific ways, includ-ing bonuses, praise, chewing out, awards, and the like. He works at giving all men recognition, belonging, security, feelings of adequacy, and challenge. This approach suits bureaucrats just as well as it does risk-seekers. It compels no acceptance of individual risks on the part of subordinates. They may, in fact, show startling improve-ment, but they may also show no improvement at all. At the end of the next period A's results are no better than before. This most often happens when M has failed to use the development tool.

Combining Motivation and Risk Acceptance

What is added to the manager's behavior when individual re-sponsibility measurement occurs? Studies by Norman Maier and others have shown that when the expectations of bosses aren't met, the simple fact is that the subordniate didn't know what was ex-pected of *him* before he started working in the period in question.

The basic step is for the man and his boss to have an under-standing in advance of the period about what the subordinate's major areas of activity and responsibility are, what will constitute a good job (or a bad one), and what conditions should exist at the end of the period if results are to be considered satisfactory on all counts.

In the absence of such standards no amount of generalized motivation can produce satisfactory results based on the assumption of personal responsibility. Where the standards have been made clear, they have strong motivating effects in themselves.

Most research on motivation has been group research, that is, research into the morale and so on of a cluster of employees. Its usefulness lies mainly in inventing policies and procedures that affect the whole group. In dealing with individual A, these may or may not be effective. The doctor doesn't consult an actuarial table to decide if patient Smith will die tomorrow. He studies Smith and his symptoms individually and in detail.

A management system should provide a framework for picturing the major factors in the situation as an integrated whole. It should be realistic. It should simplify the complex rather than complicate the simple. It should also allow for some subsystems. At its best, a management system should incorporate both inputs and outputs, impute the risks of business to individual managers and be considered as an almost self-contained whole. This doesn't exclude it from being part of a larger system, however, including the value system.

Management by objectives meets many of these criteria for a systematic approach to the manager's job. It deals with the organizational framework which is common to industry. It also relates to the larger problem of increasing the vitality and personal effectiveness of managers as well as their personal risk-taking.

Management by objectives provides an answer to the problem of determining the manager's *span of control,* that is, how many men he can manage. The answer is that he can manage as many people as he can set goals for with reasonable accuracy, can measure results for—and secure acceptance for both functions.

Management by objectives defines what *kinds of people* a manager can handle in terms of his knowledge, as contrasted with that of his subordinates. For this is a system whereby a manager can manage persons of any level of competence and education provided he knows enough about their work, first to be able to define with them accurately what goals they should be shooting for, and later to measure how well their results stand up to these goals.

Measurement by objectives determines who shall get the *pay increases* from among the limitless demands for the limited funds available in the enterprise. The increases are allocated on the basis of the results achieved against agreed-upon goals at the beginning of the period.

Management by objectives distills the complex problem of *communications* by giving first priority to the communication of job-related, risk-taking information, and treating the communications of goals and results as the primary communications problem.

Management by objectives also solves much of the problem of *delegation* by treating it as a learning curve. The rate of control can be diminished at the rate which the superior can teach the subordinate to act on his own, and the rate of subordinate independence is a function of how fast he accepts objectives and learns to move toward them.

The above list by no means exhausts the problems that can be handled by the manager who adopts the system of management by objectives. Let it be understood, however, that this is far from being a simple procedure, or a "cook book" approach. In fact, nothing is more fatal than to conceive of a management system as a cut-and-dried procedure. Experience has repeatedly shown that when the architects of a management system regard it simply as one more mechanism, it is never accepted by the people who are called upon to put it into effect.

CHAPTER 5

Installing
the System

> *How can technical change be introduced with such regard to the cultural pattern that human values are preserved? It is necessary to think about these patterns....*
> —MARGARET MEAD

Having concluded the previous chapter by warning against being too mechanical in setting up and applying a system of management by objectives, we now somewhat contrarily proceed to illustrate how such systems can be installed. The steps that will be described here have been distilled from the experience of many companies. Needless to say, they must be adapted to fit the particular circumstances in which they are to be applied.

The Necessary Conditions

The primary condition that must be met in installing a system of management by objectives is the support, endorsement, or permission of the principal manager in the organizational unit where the system is to be used. The premise that success for every subordinate means "helping his boss to succeed" means also that the boss must be in accord with the goals of the subordinate and must not oppose the methods he uses to achieve them.

Hence, the place to begin an installation is with the top man in the organization where it is to be started. If the system is to be used at the corporate officer level, this will probably be the company president. At the divisional level, it must include the general manager, if the key functional heads are to use it as a way of managing. In manufacturing, sales, and engineering departments, it must include the plant manager, sales manager, or chief engineer of each of these functional units if it is to work effectively in them.

This doesn't preclude any manager whose boss is not opposed to his using the system from going ahead on his own and installing it in his own department or unit, so long as he has discretionary power over methods of managing.

The installation of management by objectives in the national sales organization of Honeywell's Micro-Switch division, for example, was successfully carried out because the division's national sales manager decided that the system had strong possibilities for his group, and his general manager enthusiastically backed him up. In numerous other companies, personnel, R & D, and accounting departments, legal staffs, and other units have successfully installed management by objectives where the top man in the unit was free to do so, and wanted it to be done. Usually the installation proceeds through the following phases:

1. Familiarization of the top man and his key executives (those reporting directly to him) with the system and how it operates.

2. Following the decision to install the system, the top man and his subordinates program measures of organization performance.

3. Goal-setting methods are then extended down through the organization to the first-line supervisory level through a successive series of meetings between the various organizational units and their superiors.

4. The necessary changes are made in such areas as the appraisal system, the salary and bonus procedures, and the delegation of responsibility. Ambiguous policies are clarified and procedures that may be blocking effective operation of the system are amended. Other changes, such as the installation of a system of "responsibility accounting" by the cost department, are also made.

The Stages of Installation for the Individual Manager

For every manager starting out to install this system in his own activity, the questions naturally arise: "How and where do I start?"

What steps are involved?" Following is a workable procedure for the individual manager at any level:

Actually two distinct but related activities are involved:

1. At the beginning of each budget year the manager and each of his subordinates agree on the subordinate's targets of performance for that year.

2. At the end of the year they take out these targets and jointly review the subordinate's performance against them.

Let's look a little more closely at each of these activities and see what the manager does to accomplish them.

SETTING GOALS WITH SUBORDINATES

The following steps are undertaken at the beginning of each budget period for which goals are to be established:

STEP ONE. Identify the common goals of the whole organizational unit for the coming period. This is based on your desired goals for the whole organization, which are stated in terms of the measures of organization performance you intend to apply at the end of the period. Some typical areas in which a statement of common goals may be needed are:

Profitability
Competitive position
Productivity
Technological leadership
Employee development
Public responsibility
Employee relations

Usually the economic goals are stated in terms of the controllable areas of responsibility for the head of the unit concerned.

UNIT	ECONOMIC GOAL
General management	Profit
Sales	Revenues, margins, or contribution
Service	Cost of unit of service delivered
Manufacturing	Cost of product made
Staff or research	Budget and program promised

STEP TWO. Clarify your working organization chart. Sketch the actual organization of the group under your supervision showing titles, duties, relationships, and impending changes.

As a manager you are responsible for achieving organizational results and personal responsibilities. You work out performance budgets only for those reporting directly to you. Those below that level should work out their budgets with their own immediate supervisor.

Your objectives are your own goals plus the major goals of those reporting directly to you. Don't pyramid into one set of goals all the many responsibilities of all the people below you in the organization. Carry the goal-setting process to your immediate subordinates. Take individual stock of the men with whom you'll be setting performance budgets. (Review each man's past work assignment, appraisals, salary progress. Note any special factors about him and his work; his major responsibilities, what's going to be expected of him, and so on.)

STEP THREE. Set objectives for the next budget year with each man individually. Here's how you go about this:

a. Ask the subordinate to make notes on what objectives *he* has in mind for next year and set a date when you'd like to discuss these with him. Normally, these goals will fall into four categories:

Routine duties
Problem-solving goals
Creative goals
Personal goals

b. Before the meeting, list some objectives you'd like to see him include for the next year and have them ready. Note especially any innovations and improvements required of his function.

c. In your personal conference, review the man's own objectives in detail, then offer your own suggestions or changes.

d. Have two copies of the final draft of his objectives typed; give him one and keep one yourself.

e. Working from the final agreement, ask him what *you* can do to help him accomplish his targets. Note his suggestions, keep them with your copy, and include them in your objectives, if pertinent.

STEP FOUR. During the year check each subordinate's goals as promised milestones are reached:

a. Is he meeting his targets? Time, cost, quantity, quality, and service should be measured here.

b. Should his targets be amended? Don't hesitate to eliminate inappropriate goals, or to add new targets if a special opportunity arises.

c. Are you delivering on your part in helping him?

d. Use the jointly agreed-upon goals as a tool for coaching, developing, and improving each man's performance on a continuous basis. Reinforce good results by feedback of *success* when you see it. Allow a man to make some mistakes (don't hound him for them) but use his failures as a platform for coaching.

MEASURING RESULTS AGAINST GOALS

These steps are undertaken as the end of the budget year draws near:

STEP ONE. Near the end of the budget year, ask each subordinate to prepare a brief "statement of performance against budget" using his copy of his performance budget as a guide. Tell him not to rewrite the whole statement, but to submit a written estimate (giving relevant figures, where possible) of his accomplishments compared with his targets. In this statement he should also give reasons for any variances and list additional accomplishments not budgeted for.

STEP TWO. Set a date to go over this report in detail. Search for causes of variances. Ask yourself:

a. Was it your fault?

b. Was it some failure on his part?

c. Was it beyond anyone's control?

Then get his agreement on just how good his performance was and where he fell down.

STEP THREE. At this meeting, also, you can cover other things that may be on his mind. If he's so disposed, you might discuss such matters as relationships on the job, opportunity, job-related personal problems, and so on. But don't rush this. If he'd prefer, set another date for talking about these things.

STEP FOUR. Set the stage for establishing the subordinate's performance budget for the coming year.

REVIEWING ORGANIZATION PERFORMANCE
AND DEFINING GOALS FOR THE COMING YEAR

Here, of course, the manager finds himself back at Step One of the goal-setting stage, but better equipped by reason of his experience, to set more realistic goals for the next budget period.

Unfortunately, simply setting forth a stark outline of this type may give rise to the misleading impression that the installation of the system calls for no more than slavish adherence to the prescribed pattern. Actually, any mere statement of procedure overlooks the factors of time and judgment, and of the willingness to move with the deliberate speed required to overcome the cultural patterns that oppose the introduction of change.

Technical assistance teams in underdeveloped nations, industrial engineers in inefficient factories, and community development experts in rural America, have all had to learn the hard way that people everywhere cling to expectations that offer them fulfillment of the values they hold dear. In the executive suites of the nation, as in the villages of India, the natives are under the sway of gods, graves, ghosts, sacred books, and high priests. No procedure can sweep these aside with a weapon forged from the feeble material of logic alone. The procedure must allow for local customs and cultural idiosyncrasies and go forward at a pace determined by the elimination of these barriers, rather than by the dictates of pure logic.

Still, technical and logical progress must be made.

Some Indispensable Preliminaries

In installing the system, managers would do well to look to the experience of others if they wish to avoid the costs of trial and error. When, in the hope of reaping quick gains, what others have learned is ignored, a certain amount of "backing up" and redoing will almost certainly become necessary, as many companies have found in trying to shortcut some of these essential steps:

SECURE TOP MANAGEMENT BACKING

If the often-delicate negotiations that are necessary to obtain the endorsement of the top manager are omitted, the subsequent steps are likely to fail pretty badly. Unless the top man and the key men in each department know and accept what is being done, the staff man who would personally favor the use of the system might as well *defer his hopes until such endorsement is forthcoming*. It's no secret that there are many successful managers who enjoy personalized control, and don't mind at all if things appear chaotic as long as control is effectively centered in their hands. Such leaders resist systemization for a variety of personal reasons. Where they also possess abundant energy and long experience, and run the business with vigor and zest, the results will probably be good. The question, though, is whether they are succeeded by men who are their equals in ability, experience and energy. It may also be questioned whether such people are, in fact, using their talents to best advantage.

When a company is, in effect, run by one man, this usually means that several conditions exist that can hardly be considered favorable to the organization or the top man himself. He's probably tied closely to the present, and is doing too little innovation. This isn't always true, however. Many charismatic leaders are great innovators, continually pushing the organization into new—and not always appropriate fields. At the same time, the innovative powers of others may be stultified by this domination.

Most leaders who practice personalized control are prisoners of their subordinates and the job. The prisoner and the guard are both in jail. The puppet-master and the puppets are both tied to the same string.

Usually the personalized style of leadership results in the leader's working at projects below his best abilities. As a rule, these are "vocational hobbies"—things the leader particularly enjoys doing because he excels at them. Perhaps he once held the job now being done by a subordinate, and over-supervises him. Perhaps he gains personal satisfaction from a particular line of work and dallies with it, though he is paying someone else to do it. The process of weaning managers away from such vocational hobbies is in part accelerated by a systematic approach to management.

Trying to obtain the endorsement, support, or permission of the leading figure in the organization to install management by objectives will be of little avail if he resists giving up personal control. If he is intractable in accepting systemization, is successful, has strong successors coming along, and innovates, it may as well be accepted that a new system is likely to add little to the company's immediate profit and growth and had better be deferred.

In any event, if management by objectives doesn't promise to achieve some beneficial effects that can be measured, it shouldn't be pressed into use at that time.

CLARIFY COMMON GOALS BEFORE INDIVIDUAL GOALS

One of the more important reasons for involving the top leaders of the organization in the process is to engage them in setting common goals for the whole organization. This is more than a simple cumulation of the individual goals of subordinates. Such common goals may come from past history, from competitive records, from industry standards, or from higher levels of management, such as the board of directors.

Much of the literature of the social scientists who have studied and written about management by objectives has stressed "productivity" as a single measure of success. Experienced managers recognize this as but one of a dozen or so possible goals for an organization. These common goals might be in any one of the following areas:

Amount of profit
Rate of profit
Profit as a per cent of sales
Profit as a return on investment
Profit as a return on equity
Growth in assets, sales, or profit
Market position or product-mix pattern
Share of market
Quantity and quality of service provided
Productivity of people, machines or capital
Revenue levels
Contributions to profit
Employee relations, attitudes, turnover, etc.
Public relations

The necessity of setting organization measures of performance before setting individual management measures of performance lies in this simple fact:

Not all organization goals will be divisible into the personal goals of managers at lower levels.

Decisions taken at the highest level—as, for example, to buy rather than to manufacture (or vice versa); to accelerate growth through merger and acquisition; to increase productivity through automation or instrumentation—may affect the objectives of individuals in subordinate positions in a variety of ways. Individual managers at lower levels must know what these decisions are, and what limitations they place on their discretionary powers before they can be asked to propose their own goals. Otherwise, superiors may find themselves seeking opinions or suggestions that, in fact, cannot be used because they conflict with decisions previously made higher up. It is far better never to have asked subordinates to participate in decisions that affect them, than to ask them—and then ignore what they have to say.

For example, a grocery company found that its marketing methods of calling on grocers were drastically changed by the rapid rise of the food store and chain. The buyers had become more like purchasing agents of quantity lots than individual mom-and-pop grocers of the past. It became evident to top management that a complete revamping of the marketing plan was needed. Among the envisaged changes were early retirement for a substantial number of salesmen, the release of others, and the demotion of many sales managers. The pure use of participative management ("How do you think we should organize to fit the new marketing situation facing us?") produced a vast array of resistance to the drastic upheaval that was obviously called for. As a result, a great deal of bitterness ensued when the necessary change was enforced from the top. But what really irked the managers was that they had been asked their views and given them freely, had then been ignored, and had had the inevitable ill effects upon the sales group forced on them anyway.

The establishment of measures of organization performance before individual measures are set *defines the boundaries* within which subordinates can legitimately propose goals. Once these boundaries are known, individual goals and budgets should be solicited, and to the extent possible should be used to *adapt to organization goals.*

In brief, *the establishment of measures of organization performance should precede goal-setting meetings between managers and subordinates.* These measures of organization performance delineate the areas of decision of both parties in the joint goal-setting process.

While many of the measures of organizational performance will be summations of the individual goals of managers, those which are not should be clearly identified.

CHANGE THE ORGANIZATION STRUCTURE
IN ACCORDANCE WITH GOALS

The sketching out of the actual organization structure follows goals. The reason for this is similarly logical. If goals are being changed, there may be organization changes that will be required as well. In the case cited above it was the goal which shaped the organization and not the reverse. Changes in organization will lead to changes in individual areas of responsibility and authority and should be clarified before subordinate managers are asked to work out their performance goals and measures for the coming period.

THE MANAGEMENT-BY-OBJECTIVES CYCLE

As Figure 5-1 shows, the system of management by objectives is a cycle. In this cycle, the newest feature is the *joint establishment* of subordinate goals. This is also the phase of the process that requires the most time from the most people.

This use of time on the manager's part is an important aspect of management by objectives, and depends heavily upon three points of emphasis:

1. *Management by objectives is a system of managing, not an addition to the manager's job.* To return to our example of Manager M, if he is to identify common goals, restructure his organization, jointly set goals with his major subordinates (A, B, and C), and use these goals as measures of results, both for the entire period and for periodic review, he will be too busy doing all this to do much else. In other words, he will be too busy managing to do much else.

2. *The manager who adopts management by objectives as a*

Figure 5-1

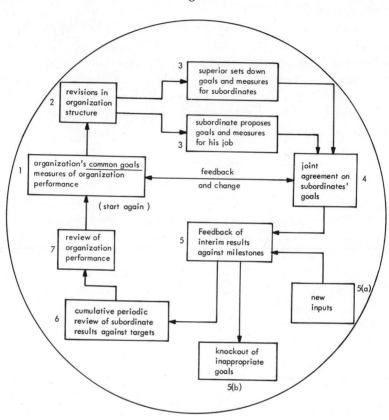

The cycle of management by objectives.

system of managing must plan to drop some of his more time-consuming vocational hobbies. This is another way of saying that the manager must delegate, or relinquish personal control of certain activities that he has hitherto personally manipulated or overseen in too much detail. The difference here in his behavior is that he adds the teaching of the subordinate to his duties, and his rate of relinquishing personal control is identical with the rate at which he teaches the subordinate to perform as an independent operator. Thus the *learning curve* for the subordinate is the *delegation curve* for the superior. His former hobbies become responsibilities of the subordinate.

3. *The system of management by objectives entails a behavior change on the part of both superior and subordinate.* The subordinate moves in a more results-oriented fashion because he knows what his goals are. His superior provides the instruction, help, and behavior that will help him succeed. The superior must constantly ask, "What can I do, or do differently, or stop doing, to help you achieve the goals we've agreed on for your position?"

WHAT NOT TO DO

There are certain key points in the foregoing procedure that can make or break the system. Here is a brief rundown of the major "don'ts":

1. Don't get involved in personality discussions. It's becoming increasingly recognized that the chart-rating type of performance review is based on unsound premises, and achieves no behavioral change of a predictable or productive nature. Confine your talk to the job, the results, and the reasons for variances.

2. Don't discuss salary and performance at the same meeting. We'll treat salary administration and how it relates to performance in a separate chapter. Suffice it to say here that the two subjects involve many different facets and should be discussed at different times.

3. Don't discuss potential and promotability at the same time as you are working on the man's responsibilities and results. Make that a separate discussion also. We'll treat that topic later on too.

4. Don't hold a man accountable for things that are totally beyond his control.

5. Don't dwell on isolated incidents at the expense of overall results.

6. Don't make up your mind about the results a man has achieved until you've had your discussion with him.

7. Don't nag. By nagging we mean berating a subordinate for his failure to do things he didn't clearly know were expected of him.

CHAPTER **6**

Measuring Organization Performance

> *Watch out when a man's work becomes*
> *more important than its objectives, when*
> *he disappears into his duties.*
> —ALAN HARRINGTON

It would seem strange to an old-style economist or business man that we should have to begin by stating that business is first and foremost an economic institution. The reason for beginning thus is simply that the other effects of the corporation and the business community as a whole on the rest of society have been so emphasized in recent years that we may find ourselves overlooking this basic limit on our measurement of business performance.

There are hundreds of burdens that the business firm must bear, we are told. Among the most frequently mentioned are:

It must produce quality products.
It must pay fair wages.
It must pay its taxes.
It must be a force for moral conduct.
It must bargain collectively with unions.
It should teach its workers to be free men.
It should assist in the defense of its country.
It should protect the property of its owners.

It should provide for the old age of its workers.
It should not demand conformity of its managers.
It should not produce and sell useless products.
It should not try to affect private lives.
It should not conspire to set prices.
It should not become too large.
It should invent and innovate.
It should not allow its employees to become immature.
It should provide steady employment to workers.
Its prices should respond to cost.
Its management should be selected for ability.
It should restrain its own power over others.

In fact, the roster of demands upon the firm and its managers, already large, grows daily. As professional managers have increased in numbers, the advice proffered to these non-owners on how to exercise their trusteeship has become more complex. A kind of inchoate legalism now surrounds the corporation which, if ignored, leads quickly to statutory legal restraint. Is there a set of standards for managerial conduct? What priorities, if any, determine which set of values ranks ahead of all the rest?

It is the premise of this book that economic survival is still the primary demand placed upon management, and that all other measures of corporate performance must follow and fit this goal.

If, in our zeal to impose new requirements upon the professional manager, we bar him from achieving the primary purpose of the business enterprise, then we lose both the economic and the social objectives by which we measure it.

Of course, few modern managers would argue that profit is the sole measure of corporate management. It will be generally agreed that once the corporation has achieved this prime purpose it must quickly assume as many of the remaining obligations as are feasible without destroying its capacity to perform.

The key issue, then—the one that makes or breaks the business firm—is how to make profit, growth, and survival its primary goals, not only for the organization as a whole, but for each individual in its employ. Hence, the establishment of measurable, overall corporate goals must be accompanied by the establishment of measure of performance for each unit of the enterprise.

Out of the single measures of total organization performance must grow the measures of organization performance for its smaller organizational units. Where do we look for such measures?

Primary Measures of Organization Performance

As a system, management by objectives requires objectives for every level of organization where some control over and improvement of performance is sought. While single organizations may have a single measure of performance (usually there are more, even for the single organization), it becomes obvious as we gain experience that the same measures won't apply to every unit. They should however be consistent with those of the larger unit of which they are a part. One schematic way of looking at measurements of organization performance is to simulate the organization chart.

Figure 6-1

This hierarchal structuring of organizational measures of performance against their own goals is accompanied by a corollary. *In management positions the measure of the manager's performance is largely the measure of his organization's performance.* The manager is measured by the performance of his followers rather than his own personality. In short, the manager is a skilled worker in organizations.

In establishing goals and responsibilities for higher-level managers, in fact, we find that the organization chart of his unit is (or should be) a fairly close proximation of his major areas of responsibility. This relationship is illustrated in Figure 6-1.

Take the group reporting to the personnel director of a company of 2,000 employees. He has a staff of fifteen in his department. He and his boss have agreed that his duties consist of: "Directing and administering the operation of the company's personnel and industrial relations policies, procedures, and programs." His organization (showing immediate subordinates only) is diagramed in Figure 6-2.

Figure 6-2

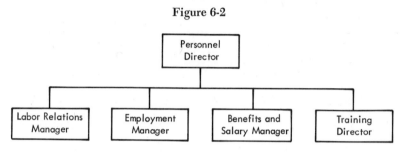

The list of responsibilities for his position would include all the major departments he directs and those things he does personally, such as advising the president on policy. If this personnel director were using management by objectives for his own position his first step might be to define his major areas of responsibility, and the measures for each:

MAJOR AREAS	MEASURES OF SATISFACTORY PERFORMANCE
Labor relations	Continuous, productive operation.
Employment	Ample supply of qualified personnel.
Benefits	Economic management of benefit programs and high employee satisfaction with their lot.
Salary administration	Equity and competitiveness in pay.
Training	Improvement in employee performance.

The actual measures of performance would, of course, include the goals imposed by the situation including top management's perceived needs, as well as the suggestions of his subordinates. Each subordinate, in turn, would define the specific responsibilities of his own position and discuss these with his boss until some agreement is reached and committed to writing.

The higher-level manager does not include in his goals all the detailed goals and measures of all his subordinates. If he did so, the pyramiding effect would soon make such a system unworkable.

Each subordinate must define the common objectives for his unit and combine them into one total. This statement of the common organization goals of the lower unit thus becomes a measure for one area of the *boss's responsibility*. In short, the subordinate has an agreement for total results and commits himself to assist his boss to succeed. What is success for the boss? If his subordinates achieve their common organizational goals, then these accomplishments combine to accomplish the total organizational goals of the higher unit.

Primary Goals and Intervening Variables

In the complex world of business, to state the end results desired is not sufficient to achieve them. The time lag between research, production, and the eventual sale of product or services is such that intermediate and early measurements of the causes of the end results must be established. Such measurements of causes differ importantly from the measurement of end results. Treatment of day-to-day affairs must be dynamic and short-range to ensure results of the next effect in line. Nevertheless, working at a causal level is always done better when the manager is aware of the end result sought in the total organization.

The first step in this process is to define the end results sought, and in economic terms that are consistent with total company end results sought. The identification of intervening or basic causal variables must await this first step.

To find useful result measurements we find some helpful answers in the field of accounting. By using the categories that managerial accounting applies in measuring performance, we can adopt some useful non-accounting aids in the assessment of managerial behavior.

THE ACCOUNTING MEASURES OF ORGANIZATION PERFORMANCE

Cost accounting or the financial statement is a basic reflection of the economic consequences of the manager's behavior. Most cost accounting also attempts to identify where costs fall in the sense of coming within the purview of the department head or unit leader. What are the three basic accounting measurements by which we measure the financial performance of managers? The newer forms of *responsibility accounting* are most germane to our purpose here.

Figure 6-3

FINANCIAL MEASURES OF ORGANIZATION PERFORMANCE

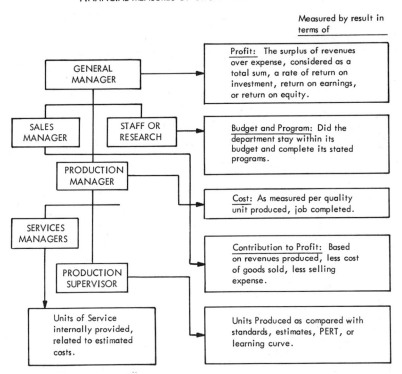

Measured by result in terms of

Profit: The surplus of revenues over expense, considered as a total sum, a rate of return on investment, return on earnings, or return on equity.

Budget and Program: Did the department stay within its budget and complete its stated programs.

Cost: As measured per quality unit produced, job completed.

Contribution to Profit: Based on revenues produced, less cost of goods sold, less selling expense.

Units of Service internally provided, related to estimated costs.

Units Produced as compared with standards, estimates, PERT, or learning curve.

GENERAL MANAGER

SALES MANAGER   STAFF OR RESEARCH

PRODUCTION MANAGER

SERVICES MANAGERS

PRODUCTION SUPERVISOR

The accompanying diagram, Figure 6-3, represents the different kinds of measures of organization performance that accounting provides. In setting objectives the use of accounting methods should never conflict with personnel development goals, and so far as possible should accelerate them. This often entails the shaping of the accounting system to one of "responsibility accounting," which means that the financial objectives for each position shown in the diagram differ from those of other positions.

PROFIT AS A MEASURE OF ORGANIZATION PERFORMANCE. Essentially, profit means total revenues minus total costs. Very few people in an organization actually have profit responsibility in that they control or affect both revenues and costs. In a small or medium-sized firm, the president is the only manager who has profit responsibility. In the larger firm, the general manager of a decentralized division may have it if he has control over both revenues and costs. In an even larger firm a group vice president may have profit responsibility for a group of divisions—again provided his responsibilities are for *both revenues and costs.*

In any kind of appraisal system it's harmful to measure a man by his profit responsibility if all he does is sell or manufacture. Profit as a result must be accompanied by control over both income and cost to be an effective measurement.

The naive practice in some companies of plastering the premises with such exhortations as "Did my work make a profit for the company today?" is often harmful on two counts: (1) Very few of the people reading these signs make profits (they contribute to them either by producing revenues, producing goods at a certain cost, or executing a program within a budget); and (2) over-attention to things for which they aren't responsible and over which they have no control can divert employees' attention from doing creative work in the areas that are indeed possible for them to influence, such as cost, quality, safety, personnel management, accounting, transportation, and so on. In any case it is discouraging for the individual to be measured against achievements that are beyond his capacity to change, control, or affect.

REVENUES OR INCOME AS A MEASURE OF ORGANIZATION PERFORMANCE. A number of people in an organization can be measured by revenues or income attributable directly to their skill and effort. These include salesmen, and members of the marketing, advertising, and sales promotion departments. In some instances the creation of *revenue centers,* with the manager in charge being measured by the revenue produced, represents an additional form of appraisal that is results-oriented. A manager in such a revenue capacity may also spend money to obtain such revenues. Thus:

Income produced
  Less cost of goods sold = Gross margin
Gross margin
  Less selling expense = Contribution to profit.

This measurement of managers in charge of revenue centers by contribution to profit is perfectly apt as an appraisal method. But it should be noted that this sales or marketing manager should not be charged with "profit" responsibility since he has no control over the cost of goods sold. His contribution to profit could be controlled by these actions on his part:

- Pushing products with high mark-up.
- Pushing items with low selling expense.
- Avoiding the sale of unprofitable items.
- Adding to his total volume without adding to expense.

COST AS A MEASURE OF ORGANIZATION PERFORMANCE. In measuring the performance of the manufacturing organization, a different kind of end measurement is necessary. Here, it is assumed that the manufacturing organization will produce a product of specified quality at a unit cost that permits it to be sold at a competitive price.

In other words, cost accounting data should be part of the final measurement of organization performance in manufacturing. These cost accounting data should be incorporated into the individual manager's goals, and the results achieved included in his personnel appraisal record as demonstrable evidence of his performance.

In order for such a move to have maximum effect on improving performance, the accounting system itself will need to be modified as explained below. Ordinarily such requirements are not part of the accountant's concern, and must be explained to him, or perhaps imposed upon him by personnel or general management as part of the latter's needs for measures of organizational and individual managers' performance.

Costs should be reported on a *responsibility* basis. That means that only those costs that are under the manager's control and to which he has made a prior commitment should be reported as evidence of his achievement. All other financial information is incidental. If these are indications that non-controllable expense has risen, or is otherwise unsatisfactory, these data should be separated from the costs the manager controls.

Moreover, the feedback should be short-range in scope. This may be accomplished by the use of accounting machines, which will speed up the rate at which reports are prepared. The best kind of cost reporting uses measures of performance which the manager himself can apply, thus enabling him to gage his own level of achievement at the time he is performing. This may require that his organization performance measures be converted into units which he can visibly see as he works.

Thus, in certain manufacturing operations, cost objectives are translated into tons or dozens of products made in an operating hour. The manufacturing supervisor can take hourly counts of his unit's output. These are often posted on charts or large blackboards where every employee can see how well he is doing. At a container manufacturing plant, for example, the cost system was based on a certain standard number of workers on the line, with a standard number of containers expected to be produced by that much labor. The cost accountant and the manufacturing manager, on the basis of the previous year's experience, machine-speed ratings, and engineering studies, arrived at the following unit costs:

Number of Workers on One Line	Total Hourly Labor Cost	Standard Hourly Prod.	Unit Costs for Labor
10	$25.00	10,000 containers	$.0025

TABLE 6-1

The superintendent of the department then converted this goal into figures that were meaningful to his foremen and workers. He placed a large blackboard at the end of the line where the containers were automatically counted before shipping.

Now, each hour an employee checks the actual production shown on the counting meter and records it in chalk on the board beside the target for the time elapsed. He also notes reasons for variances from the target, such as "No material," "Machine breakdown," and so on. Thus, in his tours, the superintendent can quickly see every hour, if he chooses, how his actual achievement compares with his target. Meanwhile the foreman, who is on the floor all the time, keeps special watch on the progress of the line. Wherever there is an offending position he at once goes there to correct it.

Not every production system will permit measurement on such
an immediate basis as this, but there are many mass-production
operations where it could be applied and isn't. The advantages are
obvious. It permits instant feedback of the results while there is
still time to make changes, before they become historical records,
and indeed before the man's superior is required to exert any kind
of pressure or direction for corrective action. Thus, self-control at
the lowest level can be achieved.

PRODUCTION BOARD Line No. 100		Crew Size: Standard 10 Today's Actual ____		
OPERATING HOUR	TARGET	ACTUAL	REMARKS	
1	10,000			
2	20,000			
3	30,000			
4	40,000			
5	50,000			
6	60,000			
7	70,000			
8	80,000			

TABLE 6-2

In quality control, the use of visual display charts of statistical
quality control which the operator has before him, and on which
he himself posts sample results, has proved to have an incentive
effect in instilling a sense of craftsmanship in the worker. It also
instills a feeling of self-control and ability to measure one's own
progress before pressures are exerted from higher up.

Such a system required that some kind of *unit cost* measurement
be developed, related to the standard of output under the control
of the lowest possible level of employee.

It should also be noted that this example applies to the container company's system of *flexible cost* measurement, since the removal of the crew from the line is a signal that only operating hours
will be measured; total volume is not as significant as the relative
productivity of the crew while they are being paid for operating
that line. It also permits the organization head to note whether or

not his *manning table* is being adhered to, or if some special condition has required that it be increased. It reports only the information that is *controllable* back to the people who are being measured. For example, the reporting board doesn't throw in information about local tax rates, plant insurance, or overhead burden.

In other kinds of work, such as the assembly of large items which may take several days, weeks, or months to complete, different kinds of control systems are required. The use of PERT or critical path routing charts and networks may serve the same purpose. These show the relative stages of completion and their sequence, facts which were agreed upon in advance, against which the organization manager can measure his performance and, more importantly, *which provide him with feedback of his own progress* at the same time as he is engaged in doing his job.

The most undesirable forms of feedback are those instances where the manager hasn't the slightest idea how well he is doing until some absentee second party releases information about it.

MEASURING ORGANIZATION PERFORMANCE BY COST

When shaping the measures of organization performance to be used for performance improvement (as contrasted with use of pricing or other financial purposes) it may be necessary to modify the measurement system and reporting procedures to fix responsibility for individual supervisors and managers according to their area of responsibility and the type of work they direct. Some general guides here are as follows:

1. The cost system should relate to the plant layout, the flow of work, and most especially to the responsibilities of the individuals in charge. Continuous mass-production plants should have different reporting systems than specialty job shops. Process cost systems (such as the one illustrated above) may differ in measurements of managers from job cost systems (where PERT was suggested).

2. *Actual costs* need not be reported to the manager in charge unless all these costs are responsive to his control.

3. *Estimated costs,* in which the cost of labor and materials, and the controllable factory expense of producing the job have been predetermined by advance estimate, should be fixed in collaboration

with the manager whose performance will be measured by the final costs that result.

4. *Standard costs* should be determined for each element; but only those elements under the manager's control should become part of his objectives in running his department. Since the standard is determined for processes before the operation takes place, the responsible manager should know what these standards are, and should have had opportunity to take exception to them for reason. Such standard costs should be stated in units and means of measurement established to permit immediate measurement and self control.

5. *Marginal costs* or declining costs for the production of additional units comprise a special production condition which should be established with the manager before production starts. The application of the learning curve to measurement of relative levels of output of specific lots or jobs should be worked out with the cooperation of the manager who will be measured by the standard. Airplane, electronics, and missile manufacturers make use of learning curves in cost estimating, scheduling, manpower planning, budgeting, purchasing, and pricing. It may also be used to assess the relative performance of managers in areas where no prior standards of an historical or engineering nature can be constructed.

PROGRAM BUDGETS AS MEASURES OF ORGANIZATION PERFORMANCE

Many subunits of companies simply can't be measured by revenues, contribution to profit, or costs related to output units. These would include such organizational units as the personnel, research, legal, and public relations departments. In such units, the measures of performance are subjective and judgmental; but they can be controlled in some respects once such judgments or policy decisions have been made:

- They can be given a budget within which they must live. This is the input.
- They can propose programs which they propose to complete. This is the output.

PERFORMANCE BUDGETING. Sometimes, staff departments, or other groups whose performance cannot be measured by revenues or units produced are assigned a fixed sum of money, and required to develop a program that will make this money go as far as possible. This kind of budgeting usually results in what Maurice Stans, former director of the Federal Bureau of the Budget, called the "equitable distribution of discontent." In a few instances it might also result in the kind of management typified by such administrative horrors as these:

- The department head asks for twice as much as he expects to get because he knows his asking figure will always be trimmed by half, no matter how worthy it may be.
- As the end of the budget year nears, the managers of the departments operating under such budgets will make an extra effort to spend anything left over, lest the surplus be taken as an indication that the total sum wasn't really needed and will accordingly be cut next year.

The only corrective for this kind of action is one in which the *program* goes before the *budget*. Under performance budgets, the manager of each unit providing staff services will consult with his superior executive, and with those who are the main users of the advice provided. Usually this will fall into three major categories:

ADVICE. In providing advice the staff department is putting its expertness to use in suggesting ways of improving the effectiveness of operations to other departments. This advice may be responsive to requests, it may be proffered without request, or it may be imposed. It may also be given to several levels or to one. It may be to top management on policy, to line managers on operations, or to other staff departments. Thus, the legal department may advise the sales department on anti-trust, top management on mergers, and the personnel department on employee benefits, all from the legal angle.

CONTROL. Staff activities falling into this category may take the form of surveillance of operations with a view to feeding back to top management, line management, or other staff departments evidence that they or others are deviating from policy. They may also consist of reporting accounting information to sales, or changing patterns of salary administration within the company to top management. Control may be exercised simply by the staff unit's providing information about itself to another unit upon which that unit can base its corrective actions. In some instances this information may be accompanied by the power to direct changes or corrections to be made without stating specifically how these things are to be done.

SERVICE FUNCTIONS. Some staff departments make and sell services provided to other departments, either at the expense of the using department, or as part of a general administrative cost. Where such service can be costed it provides a unit of measurement for assessing the unit's performance. The unit cost of service can be calculated just as the unit cost of a manufactured product can be calculated. Where such a measure is feasible, measurement is more precise. Usually this will be an estimated cost made in advance of the period and charged to the using departments at a standard rate. Thus the service staff is responsible for seeing that each service unit delivered is produced within the estimated unit cost.

Under such a system, the budget becomes an extension (in accounting terms) of the cost of delivering the promised performance. The decisions are made at the performance level when the decision maker at the general management level, having responsibility for profits (revenues-minus-costs), determines the likelihood of the program's contribution to the profitability of the firm.

Most performance-program decisions of this kind are judgmental and empirical. They are based on the estimate that achievement of the program will either improve profits for the accounting period at hand, or will enhance the likelihood of profits accruing sometime in the future. In such areas as personnel management, labor relations, public relations, or educational assistance, these decisions often become *investment* decisions and are accorded similar treatment in the mind of the general manager that conventional investment decisions obtain. The following kinds of programs are among those that might be established as staff, service, advice, or control decisions:

TYPE OF PROGRAM	ADJUDGED EFFECT OVER TIME
Management development	Continued growth and stability
Public relations	Freedom to operate
House organ	Amelioration of employee discontent
Cost accounting	Loss prevention
Operations research	Revenue increase or cost reduction

The end results of such programs can be precisely determined only through the subjective judgment of experienced managers that the programs will have the desired effects and will not produce null or negative effects in return for the money spent on them.

For the manager of a staff department then, the best and perhaps the only measure of performance is achievement of predetermined programs within budgets.

Measuring Key Variables

In this chapter the discussion has centered on the kinds of *end-result* variables that characterize different kinds of organizations in business. It's not suggested that simply knowing these end results will automatically bring about their achievement. Often, in complex organizations, the major effort of most people must be concentrated rather on some causal variable. A causal variable is one which, if diligently pursued, will contribute toward the end result being achieved.

The measurement of intervening or causal variables must always follow the definition of end results.

One of the flaws in many recent attempts to spell out the kinds of intervening variables to which management should pay attention is that they are extremely hazy about the end results they hope to achieve. A so-called intervening variable is neutral in its effect unless the end result itself is spelled out.

"Productivity" as a measure of results may be useful or useless, depending upon an understanding of what productivity adds to profit and growth. Such haziness about ultimate results breeds numerous ill effects in business. Let's take some actual examples.

The sales department of the XYZ company, for example, has always stressed *volume* of sales. All its management practices have

been designed to motivate salesmen to produce a high volume of
orders, and a rising dollar volume of sales. Yet in the year 1962 this
sales force brought in $90 million more in sales with no increase in
profit to the firm. What can we say about the motivation of this sales
force? Obviously they were responsive to the motivation of their
managers. They were consulted on how to enlarge volume. They set
high volume goals and achieved them. Nevertheless, these efforts
ultimately had a bad effect upon the company's prosperity and
economic performance. No differences were made between selling
products with a high cost of goods sold and those with a low cost
of goods sold. Selling costs were not considered as part of the sales
objectives. As a result the contribution of the sales force to profit
was extremely poor even though the salesmen's response to the
motivational actions of their managers was superb. Motivation of
itself is neutral. Without some economically sound common goals
and a clear statement of end results that comprises a good measure
of organization performance, those neutral intervening variables
nearly ruined the organization.

Productivity, for example, seems to be a measure considered to
be a suitable end result, whereas in fact it may or may not be
suitable as a method of gauging the economic performance of the
organization.

Take the ABC Company, a producer of animal feed. Management found that its unit cost per ton of feed would be lower if the
plant could run at over eighty per cent of its fixed capacity during
the year. Accordingly, it exerted pressure on the sales organization
to bring about a high volume of orders in order to utilize the plant
and thereby increase productivity. The sales department lowered
credit requirements and sold tons of fertilizer to farmers and grain
stores whose credit was shaky. While this achieved the desired result of raising productivity immensely (the plant ran three shifts
to fill all orders), the ill effects were not long in forthcoming. The
following winter, when collections began to fall down drastically,
accounts receivable were at unheard-of levels, and the many de-
faults wiped out all the profits that the better productivity was
expected to achieve.

In fact, the concept of productivity as a measure of the effects

USE THESE STANDARDS TO MEASURE PERFORMANCE OF	END RESULTS SOUGHT	INTERMEDIATE VARIABLES	SOME KEY CAUSAL VARIABLES
BOARD OF DIRECTORS	The firm will survive, grow, and be profitable.	The firm has objectives, plans, policies, controls, and is well managed in depth, has ample facilities.	Board members are experienced, proven men, show strong interest in the firm, and attention to their role.
PRESIDENT, Group Vice President OR General Manager of a Division	*Profits*, growth, market share as measured by return on investment, earnings as percentage, or return on equity.	Strong officers, capable employees, sound policies, and clean-cut goals for entire organization.	President has strong proprietary interest, creates a desire to excell, provides supportive environment to key officers, opportunities open to able, financial incentives.
MANUFACTURING AND MANUFACTURING STAFF	*Cost per unit* produced, at specified quality, as needed (in time) as measured by standards, estimated, PERT, or learning curve.	Productivity, quality standards and performance, yield, scrap, downtime, machine loading, safety, technical organization.	Skilled people, technical excellence, necessary controls, ample training, employee motivation, organization culture conducive to productivity, favorable attitudes, opportunity and incentive.
SALES AND MARKETING STAFF	*Contribution-to-profit* (revenue less selling expense) as measured by estimates, historical standard, program, or competition.	Volume, gross margin, share of market, penetration, cost of selling, advertising effectiveness, product mix.	(Same as above)
CORPORATE STAFF DEPT. (OR RESEARCH)	*Program-budget* achieves predetermined program within budgeted limits as subjectively agreed upon.	Programs, policy manuals, procedures, patents, papers, produced, installed or reviewed.	Above, plus acceptance of role and function by line department and top management.

TABLE 6-3

of motivational or intervening variables is naive in many respects. It presumes that productivity is a single measure that uniformly produces profits and growth, whereas it may have some damaging effects if the other conditions of sound economic performance are not met. The home gardener who buys an expensive power mower to cut a minuscule grass plot may well find that his productivity has been vastly increased. Unfortunately, his total cost of grass cutting has become exorbitantly high at the same time. This kind of an intervening variable merely indicates a lack of understanding of the nature of the business process and how it operates as a system.

The preceding chart indicates schematically how the respective levels of a modern corporation might be measured in terms of end results sought, the intervening variables, and the key causal variables. In terms of the common goals sought by any unit, this chart illustrates how such goals differ in the three measurement areas. It also points up the limitations of regarding any intervening variables as having universal application, and the need for shaping measures of organization performance to fit each organizational unit to be measured.

CHAPTER 7

Setting Routine and Emergency Goals

If we are concerned with the shortage of talent in our society, we must inevitably give attention to those who have never really explored their talents fully.
—JOHN W. GARDNER

With the entire framework of the system in mind, the key premise is that the goals established between the subordinate and his boss will achieve better results than chaotic or random methods could produce. In this chapter we'll deal with some of the characteristics of good goals, and some of the kinds of goals that might be set by a manager and his subordinate. We'll leave to the next chapter the vital question of the *process* of goal and individual standards setting, and how much participation a subordinate should have in establishing his objectives.

The guiding principle of goal setting is:

High performance goals are needed in every area of responsibility and every position where performance and results directly and vitally affect the contribution of the man to the organization.

The goals system should provide every manager with a means of planning and measuring his own performance and that of his subordinates. It should give him some means of knowing when he is deviating from target in sufficient time to do something about his errors. Goals should be established in areas over which the manager has control through his personal effort. There should be ample opportunity for feedback and the chance to obtain genuine satisfaction from achieving predicted targets. The system should eliminate anxiety about possible failures, when such anxiety is rooted in ignorance of what is expected.

Can Managers Be Measured Like Other Workers?

For half a century industrial engineers and motion study experts have had fairly specific ideas of how to measure the performance of hourly workers in factories. Time study, and the sophisticated methods evolved from the basic methods of measuring physical work, are quite well established. In brief, such performance measurement consists of three phases:

1. Break a job down into its component elements arranged in cycles. Each job in the factory consists of a definite series of actions which follow one another in an established pattern. Inevitably the worker goes through this cyclical pattern in his work, and each step in this cycle can be identified.

2. Establish a standard time for the performance of each of the stages in this cycle of work. Add in certain delay times as an element of the cycle. These may be for personal rest periods, delays for various predictable causes such as machine breakdown, and for fatigue as the day goes along.

3. Add all these standard times together and arrive at an average time for the cycle. This is converted into hours, and since each cycle produces a finite number of pieces of work, the standard quantities of work can be counted upon for each hour the worker is being paid. If you know his hourly pay rate you can arrive at a standard cost of production for each piece of work. This is useful in rating worker efficiency, the price of the product, and other manufacturing management considerations.

Such methods, vastly more complex in their development but basically rooted in this three-phase program, have also been ap-

plied to office clerical workers, to service workers such as maintenance men, and to other work.

The major requirement for using industrial engineering
techniques to set standards of performance is that there be a beginning and an ending to the work cycle or task, and output related
to measurable effort.

*This isn't true of technical managerial and professional work
since we are measuring responsibility and results, not effort.*

Almost without exception the application of time study techniques to managerial work has failed. If the job being studied lends
itself to measurement of repetitive cycles of work performed, it
probably isn't supervisory work to begin with. *Increased effort*
doesn't necessarily produce better results; selective choices of effort
are more important.

The attempts to measure the work of professionals such as
scientists and engineers along time study or industrial engineering
lines have been equally unsuccessful. For one thing the cycle seldom
repeats itself. Often the cycle in technical, professional, managerial,
and staff work is such that it never repeats itself; or it may be a year
or two in length—as, for example, in the work of the accountant or
auditor.

In view of the repeated failures to measure the performance of
managers on conventional time-study or engineered-work lines, it is
evident that some new methods of measuring individual managerial
and professional performance are called for. The new methods must
be adapted to the kind of effort the manager puts forth. More
importantly, they must concentrate less upon the methods the manager uses than upon assessment of the results he achieves.

This emphasis upon results or goals as the measurement of
managerial performance doesn't mean that none of the methods
used in getting there are considered unimportant. It's simply a
recognition that the method itself may or may not produce the desired results. Both research and practical experience show that the
successful manager in different situations may use different methods.
Sometimes two different methods will each achieve excellent results.

At the same time it is poor sense to measure results or performance when either of the following conditions exist:

• We shouldn't measure results that are caused by windfalls, or pure good luck on the part of the manager, and attribute these excellent results to the manager's methods or skill.

- We shouldn't rate a manager poorly for poor results if the conditions that led to them were beyond his control. ("I want results not excuses.")

Moreover, results must often be measured against a standard for which any number of persons share responsibility. Where there is joint responsibility, measurement should be against a shared standard, and the division explained. Unless the individual's contribution can be singled out from the contributions of all the others, he should be charged or credited only with a pro rata share of the group's achievement.

We know that managers in profit-making firms should be making some kind of contribution to profit. The manager who does a good job, however, may not always be measured directly, immediately, or personally by the profits his firm makes that year. It may well be that while he did an excellent job, his colleagues did a bad one. He might have done wonderfully well, but the market, the competition, the weather, or a host of other causes ran in such a way that the company lost money. Many managers declare that they work harder and smarter when the going is rough than when everything is going well for them. "When the going gets tough, the tough get going" is how one executive put it. But suppose the going gets tough, and the manager works hard and, though he is able to stave off disaster, the results are still poor compared with last year's expectations of stockholders. Should he be considered a failure as a manager?

The Assumption of Personal Risk

The initial attempt at goal setting between a superior and his subordinates often results in generalized statements of goals which do little more than restate some of the kinds of bureaucratic safeguards to which middle managers have become accustomed in their work. Typical of these evasions are such proposed goals as:

- To perform all my duties in a superior manner.
- During the coming year I will show more diligence in executing the duties assigned to me.

- It is my hope that I will personally channel my energies more effectively toward company prosperity.

Such sentiments are highly laudable, but hopelessly vague. Implicit in them also is the patent attempt to evade specific statements of results sought, and the acceptance of personal risk through being measured by individual performance.

This reluctance should be considered not so much a shortcoming of the subordinate as tangible evidence of the need for tighter establishment of results-centered leadership. Compare the above statements of objectives with these:

- During 1965, I will install and have operating a machine accounting system for this division.
- By June, 1966, I will have negotiated out of the labor agreement the clause for arbitration of standards.
- By November, I will have completed the feasibility study for the application of computers to payroll preparation.
- During this year I will have our campus recruiting brochure rewritten and ready for distribution.

Such commitments, though admittedly more risky than others for a manager or staff person to commit himself to, are more tangible. They are attached to the risk that the individual may fail—a consequence that may have adverse effects upon his chances for promotion, raise in pay, or even his hold on his present position.

In the goals-setting process the superior will find that there are four categories that can be used to characterize the goals sought. These are: statements of *routine* matters, provision for *emergency* actions, *innovative* and creative projects, and *personal growth* and development goals.

Agreeing On Routine Goals

In this chapter we shall discuss goal setting in the first two categories, leaving innovative and personal development goals for consideration in succeeding chapters.

Every managerial or staff position includes some routine duties which must be carried out. Though these are repetitive, commonplace activities, they need to be spelled out specifically for a variety of reasons:

- The boss should be cognizant of many of the small things that preoccupy the subordinate. Though the superior often isn't even aware of these routine operations, they may be important in that failure to do them well could have serious consequences, whereas when they are well done their effect is apparently invisible.
- Routine matters are often loss-prevention actions that avert the larger attention that will be needed later if they are poorly executed.
- In estimating the distribution of duties among his various staff members, the superior needs to be cognizant of this routine work to estimate the coverage of all of the facets of the operation, and the management of the time of his subordinates.
- In deciding on the distribution of the work these routine duties must first be spelled out. Such statements then form the basis for a more orderly clustering of duties to allow for their most effective performance.

Here, for example, are some typical routine responsibilities of a plant supervisor in a metal-working plant:

- To prepare the work assignment sheet daily.
- To investigate all cases of absenteeism upon the worker's return to the job.
- To maintain the supervisor's notebook, filing policies, memos and changes in procedure.
- To read and initial all time reports, inspection reports, and production reports.
- To maintain the inventory records for piece parts, and reorder from the warehouse when stocks reach re-order levels.

Such routine responsibilities may be included as part of the *job description* for the position as prepared by the job-evaluation staff. In a sense, the job description is a statement of the purpose and duties of the position, and is a charter to perform certain duties attached to it. The system of management by objectives enlarges the job description in two significant aspects:

1. All such duties are reviewed annually, and changes noted in writing. Mutual agreement on these duties is a result.

2. Measures are established specifying when these routine duties are well done.

The measurement of performance in routine duties is a two-phase process. The first phase is the prior agreement between the superior and his subordinate upon what these routine duties are. This insures more complete performance of them than would be the case if no such agreement existed.

The second phase consists of statements of *exceptions* as measures of performance in routine duties. The subordinate agrees that he is responsible for the performance of certain routine duties. He states in advance what exceptions to these routines he considers reasonable for the boss to expect.

The paymaster, for example, may report that his routine duties cluster around getting the weekly payroll out every Friday. It is agreed that the measure of exception here will be zero—in other words, the boss should expect no exceptions to the diligent performance of this routine duty. Thus, the failure any week to produce a payroll on Friday will be considered an exception that calls for explanation by the subordinate. If the cause were reasonably under his control or could have been averted by extra care or effort, the absence of the payroll will be considered a failure on the part of the subordinate.

The production manager may agree that all incoming orders from the sales department will be acknowledged within four hours, with an upper limit of 1 per cent exception. Thus, if he issues all his acknowledgments within this limit of exception, he has performed satisfactorily. If his failure to acknowledge rises to four or five per cent, and the causes were attributable to conditions under his control, he must assume personal responsibility for the failure, and explain.

Some typical responsibilities of a routine nature which can be measured by the exception principle might include the following:
- To meet all promised dates for delivery without exception.
- To issue insurance checks within 48 hours of claim filing.
- To average one pair of gloves per worker per day.
- To report all major violation reports from governing agencies.
- To operate at a spoilage level of 3 per cent, with no more than 1 per cent excess variance.

The common characteristic of these statements is a specification of an ideal condition that would exist if the routine duty were performed according to a *standard*. The measure of compliance covers what variances from the standard are permissible, and the point at which they become exceptions. If some variation is to be permitted, this is not an exception. The exception begins when the agreed-upon variance is exceeded. For such a system to work in routine managerial or staff responsibilities, two guides must be observed:

1. REDUCE EVERYTHING QUANTIFIABLE TO NUMBERS. Such responsibilities as production, quality, safety rates, spoilage, costs, and yield rates may be easily reduced to numbers, with the variances likewise stated in numerical terms. Other jobs in management do not permit such precision.

2. WHERE NUMERICAL MEASUREMENT IS IMPOSSIBLE, PREPARE VERBAL DESCRIPTIONS OF THE IDEAL CONDITIONS, AND OF PERMISSIBLE VARIATIONS. In certain areas such as community relations, employee relations, and so on, it may seem impossible to reduce the standard to numbers. Actually, this can be done more often than is believed possible. Specific key indicators may be adopted for use as measurements. For total effect, however, if quantification has been tried without success, a verbal statement of the conditions that will exist when the duty is well performed should be used.

ANALYZING ROUTINE DUTY STANDARDS
FOR RESPONSIBILITY DISTRIBUTION

Figure 7-1

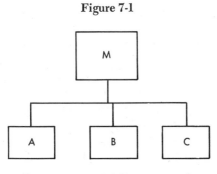

Let's presume that Manager M has received statements of routine responsibilities from subordinate Managers A, B, and C. The opportunity for a redistribution of responsibilities is worth taking at that time. Making a "responsibility redistribution" has two major facets:

1. Get statements of responsibility areas for routine duties from each of the managers or subordinates.

2. On a spread sheet lay out the distribution of responsibilities for the whole department or group reporting to you. (See Figure 7-2.)

Figure 7-2

RESPONSIBILITY DISTRIBUTION CHART			
Name Responsibility	A	B	C
Check Credit	yes	yes	no
Purchasing Material	some	some	some
Estimating	yes	no	yes
Bidding	yes	no	no

Let's presume that A is responsible for sales, B for the office, and C is responsible for the plant. As the responsibility distribution chart indicates, both sales and office state that they check credit of possible customers. A checks their standing through records, and B conducts field investigations. Manager M may choose to leave things as they are; or, if he has observed some failures in the past, he may assign full responsibility for credit checking to the office manager. He notes that all three do purchasing of certain items. He may decide to continue with this practice or come to the conclusion that economies could be made by centralized purchasing in the hands of one manager. He notes that estimating is done by both plant and sales. He may ask for a clearer definition of who does what, leaving the present system in effect, or he may shift total responsibility to one or the other as a means of insuring more effective estimating performance.

Where joint responsibility exists, as it must in many cases, specific statements as to what measures of exception should be attributed to which subordinate should be obtained in order to obtain unity of effort and to measure results of the responsible person.

So, if both sales and office manager state that they are responsible for credit ratings, some definition such as the following must be obtained from each:

SALES is to report, in advance of solicitation, new customers in order that their credit rating may be checked by the office manager. He must also report any information he has obtained in sales visits, including statements of other suppliers and the potential customer himself.

OFFICE MANAGER is responsible for credit. His performance here is measured if he maintains company membership in appropriate credit associations, checks all potential customers' ratings with such agencies, and reports these findings back to sales before any orders are taken from the new customer. His responsibility may also include sending to the sales department regular credit rating reports on all present and past customers.

SALES in turn is responsible for receiving such reports, and refraining from accepting orders from potential customers who fall below safe standards of credit. It becomes his responsibility to communicate this information to the sales organization, and to be measured by credit losses, providing he receives his information accurately and on time from the office manager.

Such a systematic analysis of responsibilities in the joint areas of responsibility demands that responsibility distributions be settled in advance of the year's program, with special attention being paid to those places where unclear definition of joint responsibility has resulted in losses or other failures to perform to maximum possible effectiveness in the organization. Some typical areas where joint responsibility exists are staff departments where sound advice and timely reporting functions may be shared with the requirements of line departments to act promptly and correctly upon information received. For example:

Industrial engineering and production
Personnel and line manufacturing management
Personnel and public relations
Traffic and purchasing
Accounting and manufacturing on cost control
Sales and credit
Sales and research
Sales and manufacturing scheduling
Production planning and assembly

The definition of major areas of responsibility and the conditions which will exist when these responsibilities of a routine nature are performed comprise the minimum standards for holding a job.

Usually such standards mean that the individual hired to occupy such a position has the required knowledge and skills to do these routine things. The individual who is placed in the position and must learn such skills will perform less than fully expected, and should be measured as a trainee, apprentice, understudy, or learner. When he is performing the routine duties according to the measures his boss can accept, then he is acceptable. It should be noted, however:

- Such a performance level might not include the ability to solve emergencies that could occur in the performance of routine.
- Routine performance may not entail much creativity or innovation in the job.
- The risk to the incumbent who levels off at the maintenance of routine levels of performance is that failure can result in removal from the job, if this failure is continually repeated or there is repeated evidence that he is incompetent to discharge these minimum routine expectations.
- This routine level of performance is the basis for nominal pay level—no higher than average—and should never be considered as meriting a bonus, incentive payment, or merit increase. Such additional compensation should be payment for performance beyond the routine.

SETTING GOALS FOR EMERGENCY ACTIONS

One of the escape valves, if permitted to exist, is the occurrence of emergency situations that account for failures to perform up to standard. Emergencies and unpredictable eventualities may be considered as ordinary in every job, in the sense that we may expect that they will happen at some time or other. The difficulty is predicating just which emergency will appear, and when. How, then, can a superior allow in advance for the time and effort the subordinate will have to divert in solving the unforeseen?

Unexpected problems arise in every job because of changes in the environment, changed demands of users of the service, the errors of others, past errors not caught in time, acts of God, or other unforeseeable forces.

The principal measure of the emergency factor in job performance is the demands the unexpected will make upon the time of the manager and thereby divert him from discharging his routine duties, or eat up the time he might have devoted to innovation.

In the goal-setting process for managers or staff persons, some estimate of emergency time required, and the needed autonomy to act are explicitly stated and time is allotted to cope with these unforeseen events.

PLANNING FOR EMERGENCIES. The effective use of management time is closely related to the amount of time that is spent in "fire-fighting," unforeseen, or unpredictable activity. Ask the typical manager and he will tell you that the things that interfere most with the effective use of his time include:

Attending meetings
Incoming telephone calls
Running meetings
Visitors
Social callers
Travel
Customers
Employees with problems

Moreover, he will add, "I can get more work done when I am alone in the office after hours or on Saturday than I can all week with the phone and other people interfering." The well-stuffed briefcase is a search for isolation to work in.

Yet, it is through the telephone, the meeting, and the personal contacts that the most effective work of managers must be done.

Furthermore, close analysis of these unpredictable interruptions shows that many of them could be programmed after some analysis of the time consumed in each.

One large firm, for example, made a study of its top staff and found that its managers averaged six hours a day in conferences, committees, and other meetings. Yet the same managers reported that the greatest interference with the use of their time was "meetings." Something is obviously askew here. If a study can show such close approximation to reality in the time spent on a specific activity then such use of time is predictable. Knowing how much time is spent on the phone, in conferences, in meetings, and the like permits them to be planned. The exact time *when* the incoming phone call may occur is mostly impossible to predict. But the prediction of *how many* phone calls the manager will receive and the total time he will consume in such "distractions" is easy. With such facts in hand two alternatives are open. The manager can begin to take steps to cut down the time he spends on these activities by doing them more effectively or he can plan the rest of his time around such schedules. In either event, if he can predict and partly control such use of his time, it need no longer be called emergency work.

The management of time requires some personal logging of time he spends in specific kinds of behavior and the establishment of other plans to accommodate these activities.

Close analysis of time utilization by categories of behavior will usually reduce the number and duration of goals proposed as "emergencies," since they have been planned.

It should be noted, though, that only the manager or staff person himself is in a good position to make estimates of the way he distributes his time among different kinds of activity. Setting goals to cope with emergencies should force some action on his part along this line.

If in performance review during the budget period, or in the periodic review of results attained at the end of the period, it is found that there has been a failure to attain either routine or innovative goals because of unforeseen demands upon the manager's time, a time-utilization study should surely become an objective for the coming period.

Many of the activities presently seen as emergencies or unforeseeable by the manager (a premise that, if valid, would constitute an escape from accountability for failure to achieve his goals) could be planned with considerable precision if a deliberate effort were made to do so.

What are some typical goals which might be established between a manager and his boss to cover the general category of emergency or unpredictable duties?

Personally investigating all customer complaints and taking corrective action.
Entertaining visiting executives from company headquarters.
Interviewing candidates for positions.
Investigating accidents.
Talking to acquaintances who call or drop in.
Coping with illnesses and deaths of employees.

A careful study of such objectives and joint discussion between the subordinate and his boss may reveal that such matters are often predictable in terms of the average time consumed, and hence should be categorized as routine, rather than emergency. When setting goals with his subordinate, the boss should try to obtain more systematic estimates of emergency activities and reduce them to routine matters. Over time, only those things which couldn't under any circumstances be predicted or estimated in advance, should be permitted to be identified as emergency, or unpredictable goals.

A high percentage of time spent in doing the unpredictable may be an indication that a lack of thorough planning has taken place, and such planning should be sought for the future.

CHAPTER 8

Setting Creative Goals

There is no hard and fast line at the point where the common sense synthesis of experience becomes a scientific ordering in a scientific system.

—R. B. BRAITHWAITE

Perhaps the greatest single area for improvement in organizational results to be attained through a system of management by objectives lies in the orderly establishment of commitments to goals of innovating, creating new methods, and introducing changes for the better into the organization.

No manager should be permitted to set goals for his position on the presumption that the status quo is good enough. The solution of perennial problems, or the introduction of new ideas to achieve better results than are presently being attained, should be insisted upon during the goal-setting process.

The right to demand such innovative or creative work has a number of related corollaries for the manager:

1. The manager who persistently fails to innovate in his own job is merely filling the maintenance requirements of his position, and, in so abstaining, bars himself from consideration for promo-

tion on merit, bonuses, pay increases other than general increases, or other advantages.

2. Failure to perform routine duties, coupled with the lack of any attempt to improve his job performance, should be the basis for the manager's demotion, or separation.

3. The rate of failure may be expected to be higher where imaginative or ambitious projects have been undertaken. The penalties for failure here should be less than for failure to perform the routine requirements of the position.

4. More opportunities for making breakthroughs or generous strides exist in some positions than in others. While this obvious difference may allow for an element of windfall or bad luck in terms of opportunity, it does not account for the differences in achievement against possible gains to be found in any position. The manager who consistently takes maximum advantage of opportunities for improvement should be handed even greater opportunity, whereas the person who sees nothing but routine work in every situation should be shunted into positions where only such demands are made upon him.

Creative goal setting in a technical, managerial, or staff position usually can be divided into one of two major categories:

Extrinsic creativity—the introduction of new ideas from outside.

Intrinsic creativity—the discovery of new ways, combinations, methods, or systems of doing the present job.

Applying Extrinsic Creativity to the Job

Not every job will lend itself to the application of new developments in science and technology. Such innovations as the conversion of record keeping to data-processing equipment, the application of motivational research to market analysis, and the use of linear programming in warehouse layout are based upon two factors:

1. Some new invention or system has been developed by others, perhaps research, engineering, or management experts outside the organization. This might be a development in the physical, social, or biological sciences, or a new management method.

2. The new technique is mastered and applied to the specific problem or problems that exist within the organization through the special efforts of an individual manager or group of managers.

The computer, the use of radioisotopes in quality control, or of operations research for transportation networks, and similar creative breakthroughs are usually introduced into an organization through the curiosity of some individual in a responsible position who tests its feasibility and installs it.

Thus William Stolk, chairman of American Can Company, is reported to have envisaged new applications of tin cans in the packaging of such products as tennis balls, beer, and other products that had not previously been considered suitable for such containers. By persistent investigation and pressure inside his organization he was able to open up new markets for the company and to advance personally. In Ford Motor Company several of the senior executives were able to advance because they introduced new methods of operations analysis and control.

It isn't necessary that the individual be the inventor of the extrinsic idea to be credited with its innovation into the organization for which he works.

Here are some typical extrinsic ideas that have been converted by one plant manager into useful and effective innovations in his plant:

The use of radioisotopes for quality control.
The introduction of statistical quality control.
The use of linear programming in warehouse layout.
The use of queuing theory in production scheduling.
An electronic order picking system in the warehouse.
Conversion of cost records to machine accounting.
Use of programmed instruction to train machinist apprentices in math.

Many more might be listed, but for this actual list, it should be noted that the method, device, or scientific principle in question wasn't invented by the plant manager at all. He simply maintained a healthy curiosity about new developments in manufacturing and elsewhere. Whenever he ran across a new invention or technique he asked himself, "Could I use this in my plant?"

Usually the introduction of new techniques or methods follows a three-step process:

1. The responsible party learns of the new idea, and *obtains a*

layman's knowledge of the technology entailed. He may read about it, attend a seminar, consult with experts in it, or visit a location where it has been applied.

2. Armed with this much knowledge, he systematically conducts a *feasibility study* to determine whether or not the new technique or device will fit into the operation of his organization. At this stage he is matching the idea with the problems, and making cost and performance estimates that show whether or not it is economical, will solve problems, or will create more problems than it solves. At this stage also, he must include some calculations of what the impact on the culture of the organization will be if the proposed change is introduced. He must predict the adverse effects that may rest heaviest upon certain groups and include plans for averting, circumventing, or overpowering these effects. Usually, he will map out methods of obtaining the support of those affected, and probe into the communications problems to be faced in instituting change. These cultural problems comprise the greatest barrier to the introduction of technical change into an organization, and are the most often overlooked.

3. The manager makes the change and installs the new method, using the insights obtained in the feasibility study. Change is sometimes introduced through testing first in a single department whose leader will be an enthusiastic and active supporter. In some kinds of programs, though, it may be necessary to make the change throughout the organization simultaneously.

The more widespread the innovation in the organization, the greater the necessity for an exhaustive feasibility study, and the greater the need for attention to the cultural patterns that might cause the introduction of the new technique to meet with resistance and ultimate failure.

Five Rules for Introducing Technical Change

Setting logical necessity aside, for the moment, we must note that the feasibility of an innovation often rests upon the manager's capacity to foresee and overcome the cultural barriers to it. Usually these require the innovator to keep five considerations in mind:

1. *Individuals will adhere to a pattern of beliefs, attitudes, and*

behavior unless something in their situation demands immediate change.

2. Technical change will be viewed as less of a change if it is *incorporated into the familiar pattern* or into an unchanged pattern of larger relationships.

3. The changing of individual behavior is a function of the individual's receiving a *series of reinforcers for small stages of development* of the new behavior.

4. The change agent who would innovate has *a wide range of methods to use in applying the new method.* For example, he may change the people; or he may change the situation so as to change the individual's perceptions of it; or he may provide the individual with satisfactions from the new method similar to those provided by the old. The mechanism of change in behavior is not one-dimensional.

5. Whenever change can be *introduced on a small scale* first and evaluated carefully before enlarging it, the innovator should follow this course. This permits careful analysis of the effects of the small change, and may avert errors that might be disastrous if the change were made in the larger dimension of the organization.

Setting Goals for Intrinsic Innovation

The second kind of innovation that can profitably be built into goal setting is of the intrinsic kind. While the introduction of new technology is important, the greatest opportunity for the working manager or staff person in the large organization probably lies in seeing the possibilities of innovation that exist in using present results as a basis for improvement and the establishment of creative goals, with commitment to such change being carried on systematically.

When a manager and his superior sit down to prepare goals for the period ahead, the time is right for the analysis of past results, and for the reshaping of goals for the coming period based on those results. The missed opportunities at this time may have an adverse effect on future results, however, if the discussion digresses into any of the following paths:

• The superior decides to practice some amateur psychotherapy and alter the personality of the subordinate.

- The superior uses this occasion to apply pure pressure, basing his action on the presumption that "motivation" means stirring the subordinate into faster action.
- The superior confines the discussion to a mutual analysis of results, instead of leading the subordinate into a more precise analysis of the situation, and the development of goals for better results in a systematic, insightful way.

It usually pays off if the goal-setting process is one that forces both the man and his boss to think deeply about the results obtained in the past with a view to improvement in the future. This usually means that an orderly series of stages of analysis is followed.

1. COLLECTION OF THE FACTS. Before the goal-setting meetings begin, each of the participants should have amassed all the facts which can be obtained about results in the past. The man and his boss probably both have some data that the other doesn't have (or which he might wish the other to know). This could include special "side conditions" and results not available or automatically presented in such formal statements of results as sales reports, budgets, production reports, or cost statements. Such collections of facts should be handled in a *classification system,* usually grouped by the area of responsibilities that cover all of the subordinates' job.

2. ANALYSIS. Breaking data down into many kinds of detail can assist in the next stage. This entails a study of causes, effects and analysis of relations. Data may be grouped qualitatively, quantitively (by statistical description) into frequency distribution, chronologically, locationally, or by dramatic instance.

3. INTERPRETATION. This is the addition of meaning to the data presented in the arranged format. What are the conclusions for next year growing out of last year's results? What do the facts or figures tell us that is new, that reinforces or casts doubt upon previously held conclusions? What are the lapses between ideal and actual, and what are the reasons for them? Problems are identified in the interpretation, and problem-solving programs are the most fruitful use of goals.

Problems are often most useful in goal setting if they are stated as questions. For example: "How can accidents be reduced from

5 to 1 per million manhours worked in the foundry?" Out of such questions and the detailed breakdown of data, *proposed solutions* can be converted into *action plans* or specific objectives to which the subordinate commits himself.

4. THE STATEMENT OF OBJECTIVES is the culmination of the analysis process, and signifies that the individual manager has now laid out his package of objectives, has committed himself to his boss to work toward them, and that the boss has accepted this as comprising suitable activity for the subordinate to follow.

In one company, a division manager received a rather terse note from the senior vice president which castigated him for one of two shortcomings in results. The statement of results was a mixture of results over which the division manager had no control, a collection of old facts that dated back several years, comparisons with non-comparable divisions, and a vague but hortatory urging to "hit the ball." In the process of installing management by objectives, the subordinate used the occasion to prepare detailed summaries of results in each of his major areas of responsibility. He dealt with cost, quantity, quality, service, and time as indicators of results. He laid this before his senior. As a result, the attitude and behavior of his chief altered substantially.

If the superior does not feel he has the available information to make such an assessment of results, he may ask the subordinate to prepare such a statement prior to the goal-setting interview. Staff services may also need to be drawn upon, to present the results in perspective to which the subordinate doesn't have access. Fact gathering should be based upon results for which there is some *evidence*. Facts are not worth dealing with in the analysis of results without some kind of tangible reference to evidence.

This emphasis upon evidence rather than hunch doesn't exclude key opinions of individuals, if such opinions affect that behavior. The self-image of the engineer, for example, has proven to be an important factor in his supervision. A fact may be considered as being supported by figures, charts, tables, graphs, statements of key people, dramatic or representative incidents, or verbal descriptions.

The manner in which the facts are arrayed becomes very significant. Let's look at two ways of arraying the same set of facts in a situation where the supervisor and his boss have the problem of setting some creative goals for the improvement of the existing situation.

Figure 8-1

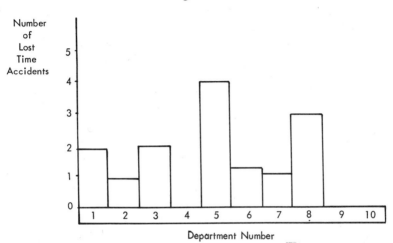

Department Number

The above chart, Figure 8-1, shows the distribution of lost-time accidents for ten manufacturing departments. A casual inspection shows that Departments 5 and 8 have the largest number of accidents. If we let the factual analysis drop here, or worse still, don't push our analysis further, we may miss some excellent goal-setting opportunities. Suppose we press even further and rearrange the same facts by order of frequency of occurrence rather than by the department number sequence.

By rearranging the order in which we present them so that those of highest magnitude are first and lowest magnitude are last, we set up a new insightful viewpoint. For one thing, we can compile a cumulative total as it goes up in major bites. As we study these facts we note an interesting relationship between location or clustering of department and frequency. The first four departments listed in order of magnitude account for seventy per cent of the accidents.

In terms of the goals of the plant manager next year, this may mean that 70 per cent of his safety effort should be expended in four of the departments.

There is more room for pinpointing targets here, however. In using such definitions of differences between cause and effect in terms of effort and concentration of energy, there's a principle that is more important than the details of this particular plant's safety record:

There is a normal and natural maldistribution among possible causes or focal points of trouble and the dispersion of effects.

To be even more specific, for every problem or for every result achieved in the past, the law of 20/80 can be assumed to be at work. This is the rule of the vital few and the trivial many among the causes of specific results. Let's illustrate this:

On the average:

80 per cent of the complaints come from 20 per cent of the customers.

80 per cent of the quality errors are made by 20 per cent of the operators.

80 per cent of the grievances are filed by 20 per cent of the employees.

80 per cent of the orders come from 20 per cent of the customers.

80 per cent of the scrap is caused by 20 per cent of the operators (machines).

80 per cent of the down time occurs on 20 per cent of the machines.

All of the above examples (of which there are countless more) illustrate this normal tendency for maldistribution between causes and effects.

In any situation where past results point to a management problem, the opportunity for improvement lies in concentrating effort on the vital twenty per cent of the factors concerned.

The Superior's Role in Creative Goal Setting

Where the principal method of trying to improve performance has been unalloyed pressure from above, the likelihood of such analytical thinking is reduced. Pressure, whatever else it may achieve, will also bring about defensiveness in the subordinate and an unwillingness to admit that he could use some advice and help in problem solving. In the face of such remonstrations or challenges as, "Why don't you *plan* better?" the typical subordinate will probably admit that he doesn't know how, and would welcome anything his boss can teach him in this area. But after heartily assuring the boss of his good intentions, and giving false optimism its due, he will most likely continue to perform at the same level as before.

In inducing creative goal setting, the superior's major role is to ask specific questions that require reflective answers, and to channel the subordinate's thinking toward constructive analysis of his own problem. The boss might try to determine if the subordinate has done any of the following things in getting at possible solutions:

1. Has he examined the facts of his situation in sufficient depth and detail to provide insight into the vital areas where he should concentrate his attention?

2. Can he rearrange his facts in new combinations? (In the above example, the facts were first arrayed in terms of rank order and magnitude and then rearrayed to show cumulative growth.) Facts may also be redisplayed chronologically, by frequency, or by geographic origin. Such simple rearrangements may reveal new facets of the problem that have previously been overlooked by scrutinizing only the original presentation.

3. Has he considered the relations between possible causes and effects as possible solutions? Has he noted changes in ratios? Has he drawn upon past experience as standards for measuring presently found results? Has he measured, for internal consistency, ideas and facts that might indicate a difference between the actual and the ideal?

Here, too, the superior might ask himself whether he has made it clear to the subordinate what the major criteria for evaluating his possible programs or goals will be?

Thus the sales manager who hopes to change the market mix of his sales effort might first explain the new pattern in terms of the total result sought for the department, and then go on to make it clear to his subordinates how their personal goals must be converted to achieve this over-all objective.

The plant manager who sees his subordinates struggling with

competing goals for cost, quantity, quality, service, and safety might spell out the major goals of the department for the year as being one or the other. For example, he might smooth the goal-setting process by stating, "The highest priority in our department this year must be given to cost reduction." Such a statement of priority simplifies the subordinate's task of attaching relative values to the possible individual goals he might set for himself.

Similarly, the research director who intimates that the major research goal for the coming period will be to "bring out more commercially usable products" materially aids the goal-setting process of laboratory directors struggling to determine whether to emphasize basic or applied research in their programs.

Some Common Errors In Goal Setting

Making a careful scrutiny of past results or present conditions as a source of ideas and points of emphasis for goals for the coming year is excellent strategy. It can break down, however, if the logical grouping of the facts, and their analysis, slips into some common errors. Here are a few of the traps managers and their bosses are apt to fall into when they are engaged in programming the year ahead:

FAILING TO ALLOW FOR THEIR OWN BIASES

Sometimes loyalty to the company or the deeply felt desire to achieve a particular goal blinds managers to conditions as they really are. This kind of bias causes the subordinate or the boss to concentrate on producing evidence that demonstrates what they believed when they started, instead of starting with the facts and asking what they have to say.

For example, the boss of a sales division wanted to achieve a considerable boost in sales. He set 10 per cent as the goal and was determined to get it. After pulling together some market analysis figures, he showed them to his subordinates as proof that the goal could easily be attained. Later, one subordinate, having gone over the same figures, said, "I've read them ten times, and they don't show a thing that he said they do. If he just wants to let me know that I've got to work harder, that's his privilege I guess, but these figures don't show any such potential in my market."

CONFUSING CAUSE AND EFFECT

The fact that two events occur at the same time, and even go up or down together in regular patterns, may be an indication that one is the cause of the other; but it might also indicate that the two sets of data are merely associated with one another and no cause-effect relation exists between them. Both, for instance, may be the result of some third cause that affects each of them similarly. Sometimes, too, the data which are assumed to be the cause are in reality the effect.

Take, for example, the statement, "Close supervision is most often found in association with low-producing departments." The manager may assume, as the social scientists have, that it's the close supervision that *causes* the low production. Yet a good case could be made for the reverse. Isn't it possible that it is the low production that has caused the boss to tighten up on his supervision of the offending department, while he leaves his better performers pretty well alone? There's plenty of evidence to indicate that in actual practice, this happens more often than not. A parallel situation is that of the man whose performance is slipping. This causes his boss to supervise him more closely, which in turn accelerates his decline. But if he is performing well his boss will leave him alone, and this freedom, coupled with his success, causes him to do even better.

OMITTING KEY FACTS

Still another form of logical error may creep into goal setting when the analysis of past results is based on incomplete facts. Some concealed event or some factor outside the data being considered may have been the basic reason for the results in question. Thus successes are attributed to a particular manager's skill and energy when actually they were mere windfalls. If his luck runs out, his results may decline, even though he does the same things once more. Selling in an expanding market is an example. The individual manager may set goals that are internally consistent, and indicate that if conditions remain the same he will attain a moderate improvement. Yet, both he and his boss may overlook the effects of a new industry moving into the territory during the coming year. Prediction in goal setting is often derived from other limiting conditions. For example: a salesman in a territory where a large defense contract covering several years ahead has been awarded should be required to submit one estimate of the effects of this upon his goals and, similarily, the textbook sales manager shouldn't be allowed to coast along on the basis of past records when it's well known that the growth in school population is going to enlarge the markets for texts at a predictable rate.

GENERALIZING FROM BAD SAMPLES

Often a small sample is used as the base for larger goals which presume that the whole population possesses the same characteristics as the sample. Thus the sales department will have a brief market study made and the extrapolated findings then become the goals of the sales manager. If the sample genuinely represents the larger population, all well and good. But if it is weighted in favor of one kind of data or one segment of the population, it can lead to false conclusions. Even samples that are large are not necessarily representative, and setting goals on such bases may be merely an exercise in distorted expectations.

One industrial relations manager, for example, set his objective as the winning of a representation election with the union. He did so on the grounds that his samplings of employee opinion had shown that the union would be defeated by two to one. But when the election was held, it went five to one in favor of the union. Why? The sample had been heavily drawn from the plant's inspection and skilled workers, who happened to be against unionization. Actually, the bulk of the work force was composed of machine operators who, in the election itself, voted overwhelmingly in favor of the union. But, because he was so certain that his goal was in hand, the industrial relations manager never really communicated the company story to the crucial machine-operator group.

FAILING TO ALLOW FOR NORMAL FLUCTUATIONS

It's actually false logic to establish targets at single points or levels, instead of regarding them as minimum and maximum ranges. This desire for a single answer fails to recognize the standard variations that inevitably occur as the result of random causes. To expect that every goal, even the most measurable one, can be precisely attained is to breed disappointment and discouragement.

"Our goal this year is to reduce customer complaints to zero." This is an unrealistic statement, which should be tempered to permit the normal and natural fluctuations around the norm characteristic of all measurement. Improvement in average performance, not perfection, is the logical limit in goal setting.

It is more in tune with logic to establish ranges of variations around a desired norm and consider anything within that range as perfectly satisfactory, rather than to set up a single figure and press everyone toward its accomplishment. In goal setting, the laws of probability should apply.

We might conclude this chapter with the findings of a study that analyzed the stated goals of 1,100 managers. The most common errors committed by managers in setting goals, according to this study, are:

1. The manager doesn't clarify common objectives for the whole unit.

2. He sets goals too low to challenge the individual subordinate.

3. He doesn't use prior results as a basis for using intrinsic creativity to find new and unusual combinations.

4. He doesn't clearly shape his unit's common objectives to fit those of the larger unit of which he is a part.

5. He overloads individuals with patently inappropriate or impossible goals.

6. He fails to cluster responsibilities in the most appropriate positions.

7. He allows two or more individuals to believe themselves responsible for doing exactly the same things when he knows that having one responsible party is better.

8. He stresses methods of working rather than clarifying individual areas of responsibility.

9. He emphasizes tacitly that it is pleasing him rather than achieving the job objective which counts.

10. He makes no policies as guides to action, but waits for results, then issues *ad hoc* judgments in correction.

11. He doesn't probe to discover what program his subordinate

proposes to follow to achieve his goals. He accepts every goal uncritically without a plan for its successful achievement.

12. He is too reluctant to add his own (or higher management's) known needs to the program of his subordinates.

13. He ignores the very real obstacles that are likely to hinder the subordinate in achieving his goals, including the numerous emergency or routine duties which consume time.

14. He ignores the new goals or ideas proposed by his subordinates, and imposes only those which he deems suitable.

15. He doesn't think through and act upon what he must do to help his subordinates succeed.

16. He fails to set intermediate target dates (milestones) by which to measure his subordinates' progress.

17. He doesn't introduce new ideas from outside the organization, or permit or encourage subordinates to do so, thereby freezing the status quo.

18. He fails to permit his subordinates to seize targets of opportunity in lieu of stated objectives that are less important.

19. He is rigid about not scrapping previously agreed-upon goals that have subsequently proved unfeasible, irrelevant, or impossible.

20. He doesn't reinforce successful behavior when goals are achieved, or correct unsuccessful behavior when they are missed.

CHAPTER 9

Setting Personal Development Goals

The job environment of the individual is the most important variable affecting his development.

—Douglas McGregor

As has already been stated, there are four major kinds of objectives that should be included in each manager's targets. Thus far, we have dealt with three of these: Routine duties, measured by exceptions. Emergency or problem-solving goals, measured by solutions and time. Creative goals, measured by results against stated objectives.

We now turn to the *personal development* goals that might be included in the set of objectives to which the manager commits himself.

The establishment of goals for the manager's personal development doesn't imply that his strictly job-centered goals aren't a form of personal development also. In fact, these job-centered goals comprise the manager's major development plan, since they relate to his job performance. Even so, beyond this, there may be personal . skills that, if acquired, will make it possible for the man to do his job better, and will stand him in good stead whether he is promoted, or stays in his present position. This kind of development may take place as the result of guided experience on the job, or through formal classes in management skills, technical and professional subjects, and so on.

How much of these personal efforts should be left to the man himself to initiate and pursue, and to what extent should his boss intervene to spur him on?

The Self-Made Man Revisited

Since the turn of the century it's been increasingly possible for American men and women of average parentage and endowments to acquire managerial positions of great responsibility. Most auto executives, we're told, come from humble backgrounds, and the story of the youth of modest beginnings who rises through the ranks to head a great corporation is a beguiling and commonplace one.

One result of these enticing prospects for the youth of modest origins is that many middle and lower-level management people are today engaged in a frantic scramble to improve their status and rank through "self-development." Corporate management-development programs have encouraged this scramble to a large extent by piously proclaiming that "all management development is self-development." A further consequence of this movement has been a sort of crusade that has led thousands of frustrated young men to cultivate the skills of self-denial, leaving them self-absorbed and all too keenly aware of the sacrifices they are making in order to get to the top.

The trouble is that when self-development becomes too introspective, not only does it often fail in its immediate objective, but almost invariably, it also fails in its ultimate objective.

Can Behavior Be Changed?

William James is reported to have said that by the time a man has reached the age of thirty, his basic habits and personality pattern are fixed and he probably will retain the same general configuration for life. Psychologist Robert McMurry has developed a most ingenious selection procedure on this thesis. It employs the "pattern interview" in which two basic patterns are used.

The first pattern is derived from a group of questions about the individual's background. After putting these questions to a large number of people, the interviewer is able to detect a pattern among the answers. The second pattern emerges in the analyzing of individual responses. The habits and attitudes thus revealed point to a particular configuration of personality which is quite useful in predicting the individual's future behavior. According to McMurry, "the pattern interview can be the equivalent of a long and personal acquaintanceship with a person." From the underlying logic of this approach, he has generalized that fundamentally "people don't change." A man's future is thus based on a sort of one-two combination that will govern his place in life; a combination of *good genes and good luck.*

Others hold that this line of thinking isn't true at all. The essential nature of man, they assert, is his capacity to improve. The American dream is based upon what de Tocqueville called "the perfectibility of man." The distinguishing quality of humans, this school of thought maintains, is the educability of man and the capacity of the human mind to enlarge its knowledge. "Man," says anthropologist Ashley Montagu, "is the most plastic, the most malleable, the most educable creature in the world."

This latter viewpoint underlies many of the programs of self-development. Its optimism and idealism are naturally more attractive to the ambitious than the gloomy views of the people-don't-change school. Moreover, anyone who has had experience with the young knows how educable they are. On the other hand many managers can point to large numbers of workers, line supervisors, and middle managers who have become fairly rigid, except that, as they will ruefully admit, "they sometimes get worse."

Perhaps the basis for self-development lies in retaining the human qualities that keep one educable. That this educability is widespread—more so than is sometimes conceded by the pessimists—is evidenced by the prevalence of adult education. Why do some people never lose their zest for living and learning, while others live careers of static repetition? It is probable that this is more a function of the environment than of the man himself. Continued success through self-change and self-development breeds more of the same. But where such effort is unrewarded, it dies.

Self-insight isn't enough, then, to assure self-development. Certainly it shouldn't lead us to conclude that self-inspection always leads to self-understanding. Such self-understanding is more apt to come through looking outward—to the study of others—than from prolonged scrutiny of one's own interior. Man is the best mirror of man, and in learning about others we understand better about ourselves. This is especially pertinent for leaders. In any event, in studying others we at least learn how to behave productively in society, even when we don't learn about ourselves.

From this set of premises we can now proceed to note some common fallacies in many of the self-development plans of aspiring executives.

Because so many management-development programs have failed to bring about any significant change in the behavior of the trainees, many experts have despairingly concluded, "After all, it's up to the man." This has provided the rationale for a science of self-development in which the successes can be attributed to the process, and the failures laid at the door of the individual himself. The trap here is the assumption that, by directing his energy and passion *inward*, the man can master his outward environment. Success, as we all know, depends partly upon outside circumstances and partly upon oneself. In fact, the ability to move away from unfortunate circumstances may itself account for the majority of success stories. Where this option does not exist, a man's upward progress in an organization may sometimes be accounted for by his capacity to change the limiting conditions to fit his capabilities.

Lastly, there is the elective of changing oneself to fit the environment, through some self-imposed therapy upon one's own inner experience. This is a miserably weak strategy, however, for two reasons. First, because he is absorbed in observing himself, the individual lacks the perspective of an observer outside the system he is trying to adapt to; and second, because outward behavior doesn't always resemble the inner experiences that accompany it. No science of self-development based on this mirror-gazing can possibly work. Where the organizational environment is at all favorable to his rising in it, a man will succeed far more readily if his education, adjustments, and energies are directed *outward*, not dwelling perpetually on himself.

The successful man is one who has objective interests which absorb him, thus making him an object of interest to others.

The Myth of the Executive Personality

At the heart of many of the self-development plans of eager young men is the false notion that there is an ideal executive personality which is equally effective in any kind of organization. To date, however, despite the most intensive search, nobody has been able to find one. There is no single personality trait, and no combination of traits which is always present in the successful executive and always missing in the one who doesn't make it. Let's test this in a simple way with the most commonly held illusion in this area:

Initiative is often thought of as a quality that every successful executive must have. Nothing proves it. Many executives rise and do a fine job as executives without it. Some inherit the business, reluctantly decide that their duty calls for them to devote their best efforts to it, and succeed. In other cases, the executive himself doesn't have any initiative, but his wife has it for him and she prods him into moving upward. (She got it from her mother!) Sometimes, initiative plays no part in a man's success at all. The fact was that he happened to be in the right place at the propitious moment and honor and responsibility were thrust upon him. A similar analysis can be made for any other trait.

The principal reason why a particular personality trait (or any combination of traits) can't be used as a discriminatory measure is that executive performance is more often a combination of *actions* taking place within a *situation*. Self-development is the readiness and the ability to take action that suits the situation of the moment.

In fact, business leadership and responsibility can be regarded as both a container and the thing it contains—the container being the organization and its setting, and the contained, the manager.

To use another analogy, clearly the scene encompasses the actor. The motions and words of the actor—his managerial behavior —must be consistent with the scene or they become comic and awkward.

The kind of self-development in which the manager labors at cultivating a shut-in "executive" personality is not only useless, it also limits his ability to follow stage directions. It causes him to ignore the environment toward which his behavior and development must be attuned if he is to sustain his part and earn the right to be cast in even larger roles. This analogy doesn't mean, however, that the actor is without significance in the scene. If managers did not have an impact on their environment, then managerial self-development would merely mean the acquisition of chameleon-like qualities, and the manager in a bad company would automatically become a bad manager, making no effort to bring his personal qualities of superior action to a poor scene.

Yet, as the professional actor soon learns, the faculty of selecting good plays (with good scenes) is just as important as the ability to faithfully enact the part prepared for him. So, in business, choosing an organization that matches one's skills and abilities is more important than cultivating a repertory of personality traits to be applied regardless of the environment.

Since success is a combination of leader, followers, and situation, a sure-fire leadership personality is impossible to define. Being impossible to define, it's impossible to develop.

The Limits of Classroom Methods of Personal Development

The marvelous confidence of American educators in the power of the classroom teacher to remake the world is a refreshing phenomenon. Unfortunately, it's an assumption that's seriously open to question. Much can be achieved in the classroom, of course. Verbal behavior, and perhaps written behavior also, can most certainly be changed. This is what happens in most college classes, and in the formal school system. The graduate can now speak and write about things that he could not speak and write about before; or, if he could, he can now do so with greater facility. Laboratory courses teach him other kinds of behavior that he can repeat elsewhere. There's quite a respectable list of various kinds of managerial or professional behavior that can be wholly taught in the classroom (that is to say that when he is back on the job no special supporting conditions are needed for the man to apply what he has learned). Thus, managers and professional employees can be taught in class:

To make speeches
To lead conferences according to a method
To write better technical reports
To interview another person
To write better business letters
To perform mathematical calculations
To program a computer

The reason we know that behavioral change can take place in such areas is that identification of the end behavior sought from training is almost wholly under the control of the instructor and success or failure can be measured inside the class itself. Consider, however, the accompanying diagram (Figure 9-1).

Figure 9-1

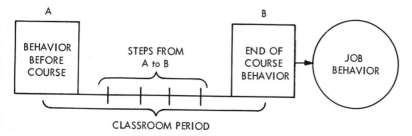

Here, we are no longer concerned with the kinds of behavior that are susceptible to change within the control system of the classroom and the instructor. Now we are considering those kinds of behavioral changes that have significance only if they are carried over to the job. Among such behavioral changes are:

The manager delegates more.
He makes better decisions.
He seeks out subordinate viewpoints.
He works through committees.
He conducts a cost-reduction program.
He solves grievances better.

Such activities can be taught up to the point where the trainee *discusses* these topics in the classroom; but any actual change in his behavior is beyond the control of the classroom instructor or of the class method of teaching. The classroom training becomes merely one of a variety of forces that reinforce or extinguish behavior on the job. Let's look at job behavior and see some of the other kinds of forces that may determine whether a man changes his job behavior or not as a result of what he has learned in class.

Figure 9-2

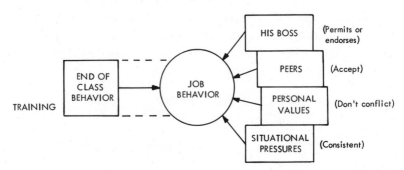

1. If he has acquired *new knowledge,* as a rule he won't lose it back on the job. But if this knowledge is rather complex and technical, he may find it fading away from disuse if he doesn't use it. Whether he applies it, however, may be more a function of his responsibilities and duties than of the effectiveness of his class teaching.

2. If he has acquired *new attitudes* in the class, and measurement of his behavior at the end of the course shows that the class has affected his attitudes, these may persist, or they may fade away or be extinguished on the job. The fading away or extinguishing of newly acquired attitudes can result from their unfavorable reception by his boss or his peers, second thoughts about the course, in comparison with certain values he finds useful on the job, or steady situational pressures.

3. If he has acquired *new skills,* he may use these on the job, provided they don't conflict with the boss's ideas of correct behavior. He may use them, so long as this doesn't mean flying in the face of his peers and flouting the cultural pattern of acceptable behavior. Their use must be consistent also with the situational pressures in

his work. Any or all of these forces may work to overcome the man's inclination to use his class-acquired skills on the job.

Here's one example of the limitations of classroom instruction.

Several manufacturing managers from a large firm went to an evening course at a local university. The course instructor, a professor of psychology, was an advocate of group decision making and the supervisors readily learned how the procedure worked. In role-playing sessions in the class they demonstrated their ability to follow it. Then they went back to their jobs, where all their people were closely tied to their machines, which were of the continuous-process type. When a problem came up, managers had to make snap judgments, with little margin for error. This they were able to do most of the time because they all had long experience on the job and few questions arose to which they couldn't quickly come up with an answer that worked perfectly well. As a result, they never used group decision making in their jobs.

One of the most common experiences of industrial trainers after conducting a supervisory course and distributing evaluation cards for the trainees to fill out is to be greeted by the overwhelming response: "Why don't you give this course to my boss? He never does any of these things."

Such a response probably means that the skills imparted in class won't be used on the job. The trainer might have averted this by doing one of these things:

1. Teaching the subordinates their boss's favorite method of managing.

2. Holding the course, perhaps in briefer form, for top management and getting their acceptance for the subject to be taught to the lower-level managers. If permission for or endorsement of the proposed course isn't forthcoming at the end of the top manager's course, the trainer should not offer the course to the subordinates. If he does, he may expect one of two results: Either the supervisors will behave in a way that their boss disapproves of and perhaps be rated low because of it, or they will acquire one kind of skill and be forced to practice a different kind. This will lead only to frustration and disappointment.

Here are some guidelines for insuring the success of a management training course:

1. Confer with the top manager of the unit in which the managers are to be trained or taught. Spell out the kind of behavior change aimed at, and make sure he is willing to accept it.

2. Give the top management of the organization a brief preview or summary of the course, if not the whole course, before giving it to the subordinates. Ask the top managers to endorse the new behavior, or even to start practicing it.

3. At the same time as this top management endorsement and participation is obtained, the environment in which the supervisor works should be studied to see whether or not the proposed new behavior is consistent with it. This can be done by visiting the proposed trainees, and noting the conditions of pressure, time, cost, quantity, service, and discipline under which they function. If these conditions appear to be unsuited to the kind of training proposed, it is better not to offer the course.

4. Give the course to the lower-level managers and obtain the cooperation of higher management in reinforcing application of the training back on the job. This can be done by checking on the part of the superior, or feedback from him—telling his subordinates that he has noted the new behavior and approves of it.

5. Action types of training that involve the learner in simulations of situations he will encounter back on the job make the carryover to the job easier. Role playing, case studies, management games, and the like can all help to bring about behavioral change. They need to be accompanied, though, by discussion and critique.

The Goals of Personal Development

A manager's personal development goals will usually comprise only a small segment of his total objectives for the goal-setting period. Exceptions to this might be younger men or women whose primary responsibility is to learn—such as being a trainee. The working manager, however, will probably limit himself to two or three self-development goals. Here, he has a somewhat bewildering selection to choose from:

The completion of courses toward a degree in evening college
Attendance at two seminars a year
Membership and active participation in a professional group
Subscription to two or more periodicals
Completion of adult education courses
Completion of company training courses
Attendance at an advanced management course
Carefully planned visits to other plants or offices
Visits to customers or supplier plants and offices
Participation in one or two community service activities
Serving on high-level committees inside the company
Special assignments in other areas of the business
Covering another department during vacation
Conducting special investigations
Participation on junior boards or functional committees
Personal health-building programs (with medical advice)
Conducting training classes for his own subordinates
Teaching adult education classes or evening university courses
Being a guest speaker at university classes
Being a seminar leader for a trade association
Writing a paper for a professional publication
Reading a specific number of management books
Preparing special speeches or presentations for an executive
Serving as secretary of boards or management committees

From this list, which for some individuals could be extended
still further, it's evident that some managers could spend most of
their time on this kind of thing. In fact, a small number of managers do spend an inordinate amount of time on such activities.
They are perennial attenders at courses and seminars, and often
concentrate on these self-development efforts at the expense of performing some function of direct value to the company.

While the training staff man may find himself attending many
meetings to determine their worth for other members of the organization, the operating manager in manufacturing, sales, or general
management positions, should limit himself to no more than three
or four. In any event, if personal development activities are to serve
any real purpose, the following rules should be observed:

1. There should be a specific reason in mind for undertaking
the activity.

2. The effect of the desired change in behavior on the man's job performance, either present or potential, should be weighed.

3. A commitment in writing, stating when these personal development goals will be completed, should be obtained from the subordinate. This statement should be specific in terms of what is to be done, when it will be completed, and the general approach or method to be used. There should also be some indication of how the boss can measure the results.

4. The subordinate should be asked for some kind of follow-up. This can take the form of either a written or an oral report on the progress he is making toward his self-development, and how this progress relates to his work performance.

How Much Subordinate Participation in Goal-Setting?

The only purpose for which power can be rightfully exercised over any member of a civilized community against his will is to prevent harm to others.

—JOHN STUART MILL

Among academic students of management, there is much controversy over the question of how much autonomy the subordinate should have in shaping his own goals, as well as those of the unit in which he works; and how strongly the boss should impose his views when it comes to goal setting with subordinates. We'll deal with some of the key issues and ideas on this question in this chapter.

Because participative management has been extensively studied, parts of this chapter will be supported by citations from research on this subject. Those who are averse to detailed recitations of research findings or are already fairly familiar with the studies in this area can skip to the table on page 144 where the major findings are summarized.

In essence, at one extreme is the position that subordinates should be asked to set their own goals and those of their work unit. The rationale for this approach, according to its advocates, is that it motivates subordinates to do more, or be more productive. At the opposite pole are those who take the view that if the boss doesn't know what he expects from his subordinates, he shouldn't have them on his payroll. He therefore should *tell* people what to do, and when and how to do it.

Actually, neither extreme is a universally applicable style of management, or of goal-setting.

Close scrutiny of the research itself leads us to the conclusion that the researchers who conducted these investigations may not be the best authorities to prescribe how their findings should be used. In any case, the research evidence indicates that the use of participative management is a discriminatory skill. In short, it shows that participative management works with some kinds of situations and followers, and does not work with other kinds of situations and followers.

Which kind of situation will probably call for participative goal-setting, and what kind calls for "tight technical organization, tight discipline, and effective control from above"?

The system of management by objectives has been hailed by the advocates of "power equalization" because of the possibilities it holds for the exercise of participative management. Now it's true that participative management is perfectly acceptable as one method of goal-setting in the management by objectives system. As a system, however, management by objectives works also by autocratic or top-down goal-setting. The choice of which method to use, or when to mix them, is determined more by the demands of the situation, especially the *expectations of subordinates,* than by the basic nature of the system itself. In fact, the system is really neutral to such value judgments.

Let's look more closely at the system as it might demand either participative or autocratic methods, or mixtures of the two.

Let's go back to our old friend, Manager M, with his three subordinate Managers, A, B, and C. The organization run by Manager M exists for a purpose: the accomplishment of certain objectives for which the members of the group were hired. These people are aware that this purpose exists, though its exact specifications may have become blurred by each individual's preoccupation with the mechanics of his specific task. Ultimately, somebody will evaluate the performance of the group by comparing how closely its results match the goals it was formed to achieve.

Here we have a type of system commonly found within administrative units. In fact, it could be argued that it is a basic system. Schematically it resembles Figure 10-1.

Figure 10-1

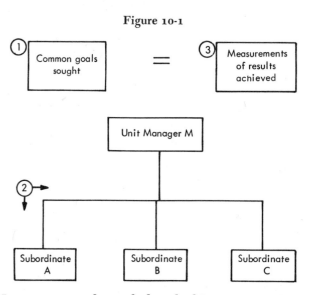

1. In *common goals* we find such things as organization purpose, policy, objectives, plans, and aspirations common to the whole unit. These include budgets, standards, programs, projects, PERT, networks, and so on.

2. In *manager-subordinate relations* we find such matters as review, control, appraisal, management by exception, the annual business review, closing statements, budget reviews, periodic cost statements, production reports, volume reports, and the like. Let's look at this whole area in some detail.

The Research Findings

Social scientists have done extensive research in the subjects of leadership, organization, and communications. Some of their discoveries have been widely hailed as breakthroughs in management, or new patterns that will eventually supplant existing methods of managing. Most of this work has been extended to the prescriptive conclusion that participative goal setting is better than nonparticipative goal setting.

Actually what have the social scientists learned from their research? One provocative idea they have suggested is that participative management obtains better results than autocratic control and dictatorship. This question will be dealt with in this chapter.

Perhaps the leading exponent of participative management has been Douglas McGregor. In describing how management by objectives works he says:

"Genuine commitment is seldom achieved when objectives are externally imposed. Passive acceptance is the most that can be expected, indifference or resistance are the more likely consequences."

If this statement is true, unqualified by any *situational* side conditions, or is borne out by the research evidence, then management by objectives is far more complex than we have supposed to date. The methods of managing that have worked quite effectively in industry thus far have really been shadows of the potential that might have been achieved if superior methods had been used in identical circumstances.

Just what does the research tell us?

Unfortunately, the popularized versions of this research have implied that the findings are generalizable to *all kinds of man-boss situations, and at all times.* Yet a careful reading of the original studies shows that the researchers themselves are often less general in their claims.

Likert, for example, reports that in a *service operation* in the early 1950's "where men are free to set their own pace, their department is probably higher-producing than where closer supervision exists." There is no assertion of a cause-and-effect relationship at work here. (As we have already pointed out, low-producing departments are apt to be more closely watched, while higher producers are apt to be left alone.)

Studies by Metzger (1956), Gerard (1958), and Pelz (1957) show that scientists who set their own goals are higher producers than those who don't. Danielson (1960) explains this in terms of the self-image of scientists and engineers. Scientists, he reports, have a higher desire to choose their own projects (set their own goals) than do engineers, who are perfectly willing to work at another's goal provided they know what's expected, and what the limits are, and are then free to work by their own methods. According to Pelz (1957), daily contact with the boss combined with independence in method increased the productivity of scientists.

A study of insurance agents by Likert and Willets (1940) found, however, that they were less productive when left entirely to themselves, even though they were working on commission.

Kahn, in a study of a clerical operation (1956), found that high goals, and an enthusiastic boss who showed a lot of interest in his people led to high productivity.

Seashore, studying an organization whose personnel were not identified, found that low producers get pressed, high producers do not. Katz (1950) found that clerical workers in lower-producing departments were under closer supervision than workers in higher-producing departments.

In railroading, Katz, Maccoby, Gurin and Floor (1951) reported that high-producing foremen tended to ignore the mistakes of their men, whereas the low-producing foremen punished them. Presumably there were more mistakes in the lower-producing units —an assumption that ties in with the results reported by Seashore, Likert, and Katz. It also checks with the experience of managers who know that when things are going badly they will bore in harder, move things around, try to find out what's wrong, and make corrections. If things are going well, only the inexperienced or naive foreman becomes a second guesser or a bird dog.

Gurin, Veroff and Feld conclude that participation is really a middle-class value, and grows out of the prior expectations of those being supervised.

Vroom has pointed out two distinctions in the definition of participation. The first he calls "psychological" (the person thinks he is participating in the decisions that affect him), and the second, "objective" (he actually participates strongly in the decisions that affect him whether he knows it or not).

Vroom's study throws some interesting light on how follower personalities affect participative management.

"The effects of participation in decision-making depend upon certain personality characteristics of the participant," Vroom says.

Summary of Researches into Effects
of Supervisory Practices in Differing Situations

RESEARCHERS	DATE	TYPE OF SITUATION	FINDING
Likert	1950	"Service operation"	Men set their own pace . . . high production found.
Metzger Gerard Pelz	1956 1958 1957	Scientists in research organizations	Scientists who set own goals are higher producers than those who do not.
Likert and Willets	1940	Insurance salesmen on commission	Insurance agents left to themselves are less productive than those being contacted more often.
Kahn	1956	Clerks in insurance offices	Bosses with high goals, lots of interest in workers, and enthusiasm have most productive units.
Seashore	1950	Not known	Low producers get pressed by boss, high producers do not.
Katz	1950	Clerical workers in insurance	Lower-producing workers are under closest supervision.
Katz, et al.	1951	Railroad laborers	Low-producing foremen punish more mistakes than high-producing foremen.
Vroom	1960		"Effect of participation depends upon personality of the participant."
Patchen	1962	18 factory groups	Close supervision, combined with high rewards and cohesive groups, produced high results.
Rubenowitz	1962	Swedish railway workers	"Production-oriented supervisors rated higher in overall performance than" people-oriented supervisors.

TABLE 10-1

For example, independent people perform better when they have high participation, his research shows.

Highly authoritarian personalities, on the other hand, perform better when they don't have any participation, but are simply told what to do, when to do it, and how to do it.

Almost everyone *likes* participation, however, even though his productivity may not be favorably affected by his getting it.

How can we explain these conflicting data? According to Vroom, it's because we like things that meet our needs. If a person likes participation, participation is what meets his expectations and needs. But some people, unfortunately, have never been led to expect that they will be asked to participate in the decisions affecting them.

The difference in the effects of tight or loose supervision, of participation or nonparticipation, is shown in the recent studies by Martin Patchen, of the University of Michigan, which found that close supervision, combined with high rewards or exercised in a situation of high group cohesiveness, resulted in high production. In still another study of a Swedish railway system, Rubenowitz (1962) also found production-oriented supervisors rating high on overall performance, whereas "person-oriented" supervisors rated lower. The findings of these two studies are thus diametrically opposed to those of earlier studies using comparable methods on similar kinds of workers.

The conclusion to be reached is that neither tightness of supervision nor looseness is a sole controlling variable, and that participation of itself has no claim to being the core of a new pattern of managing that will guarantee high productivity if universally adopted by managers. There is some evidence, however, that a strong orientation toward goals, coupled with leader enthusiasm, ample rewards for achieving them, and the uniting of people in moving toward them, does have a beneficial effect.

If this be the conclusion of the social scientists, all it tells us is that what appeared obvious to the good manager in the past was right all along.

Advantage of Participation in Managing Managers

In dealing with a system, such as management by objectives, designed to cope with the problem of managing managers, it would be erroneous, however, to brush participative management aside. It is most useful under the following circumstances:

1. Where subordinates expect that they will have an opportunity to participate in the decisions affecting them, or in setting their own goals. To bar such participation would clearly be unproductive.

2. Where the subordinate manager already has shown himself to be of an independent temperament. Such a man will expect to participate in establishing his goals.

3. Where one member of the group has proved to be habitually inattentive to his work, careless in his relations, or productive only of foolish suggestions. Here the influence of his peer group can be brought to bear on the problem of changing the offender's behavior by confronting him with the organizational value system, or cultural value system, that surrounds him and against which he offends.

The values of peers comprise standards by which the individual will usually measure his own behavior and, if necessary, adapt to them. One way to raise the standards of the back-slider up to those of the group is to confront him with these group standards in a system staged by his superior or by the circumstances of group management. Cues, reinforcers, and other stimuli to changed behavior come from the group, the boss, and from within the individual himself. Usually the inward forces are importantly affected by the outward ones. These outward stimuli to excellence may be internalized if they are made apparent to the individual. His goals will rise to meet the expectations of his boss, his peers, or the organizational culture.

The Social Values of Participative Management

In the early days of the movement toward more participative management, the social scientists were often heard proclaiming the democratic values of permitting workers to take part in shaping the decisions affecting them. But this particular line has practically been abandoned by the new "behavioral scientists" who have steered their studies in the direction of proving that participative management increases productivity.

To many managers, it has seemed that this change in direction has been rather fruitless, and all the more so because the democratic argument did not deserve to be dropped anyway. For the company making a profit or in a sound market position, the idea of using participation for the purpose of creating a stronger society is not perhaps so outlandish as many social scientists apparently expected businessmen to think. The modern corporate manager, in fact, is often the leader in such matters as race relations, participation in governmental and civic affairs, the hiring of the handicapped, and the strengthening of the free institutions of our society.

Since research evidence shows that participative management probably does no harm, and often helps, especially in managing people from middle-class backgrounds and similar value systems, the appeal that there may be long-run social value in participation has not fallen on deaf ears. In this sense many business managers lead the social scientists in their confidence in the values of participative management, even though they may doubt its efficacy as an infallible spur to productivity.

Does Participative Management Raise Productivity?

Since it is the behavioral scientists who have argued the case for a universal style of participative management on the grounds that it leads to increased production, their position calls for careful examination. Because their data can be interpreted as showing that, in most cases, participative management probably does no harm, coupled with the fact that it offers social values in which business should be interested, it can be assumed that it is wise for the manager to try it first, in preference to more dictatorial methods. It should be recognized, however, that this is hardly a strict application of science in the modern sense. It is based largely on Aristotelian logic rather than on science of the post-Gallileo type.

1. *It is heavily weighted with values,* such as power-equalization and democracy-at-work, which are ethical and normative, rather than scientific.

2. *It is heavily weighted with abstract classifications,* such as Theory *X* or Theory *Y*, autocratic versus participative management, permissive versus dictatorial, and similar hot-cold, black-white opposites.

3. *It relies on dubious generalizations.* Studies made in research laboratories and insurance companies have been extrapolated to apply to infantry platoons, foundries, automotive assembly lines and machine shops, even though the evidence may not justifiably be thus extended.

In order for this new behavioral science to be completely relied upon as scientific in the modern sense, it should meet some of these requirements:

1. It should constitute a system that takes due account of the other phenomena commonplace in the management job and function. For example, most behavioral science theories of managing exclude the economics of the firm. In one of the leading works in the field, the word "profit" is not mentioned at all.

2. Such polar opposites as good and evil, X and Y, should be enlarged into genetic concepts that would eliminate rigid classes of behavior on the part of managers. It should be recognized that management practice is never all black or all white, but multihued, and may be classified according to the conditions that determine the dynamic relations of the manager to his environment.

3. Behavioral science research should be more concrete in terms of the company studied, who was involved, at what time, what transpired, and what actions were taken with what effect. Well-prepared, detailed case studies are more scientific, in the modern sense of the term, than surveys in which the subjects are isolated from the concrete realities of their situation.

Measured against the above criteria, the school of behavioral science that views motivation in terms of need fulfillment emerges as thoroughly Aristotelian and in many respects unscientific. How can the tests of modern science be applied to such concepts as the "needs" of individuals? A commonly held viewpoint of this school is that these needs comprise a hierarchy which ascends from physiological and safety needs through social and ego needs to the needs of self-fulfillment. But once the scientist moves away from physiological needs (which can certainly be measured), how does he meas-

ure the remaining needs in the hierarchy with any degree of
precision and certainty? The questionnaire and interview (perhaps
checked by adroit design, or even the polygraph) may possibly fur-
nish crude measurements, though these are likely to be distorted by
ignorance, self-interest or other bias. Nevertheless, a certain cir-
cularity of logic entraps the scientists and the subject.

*The ego needs of subjects are reflected in the answers they give
to questions. The questions also are used to measure these needs.*
No further objectivity is possible.

At the other extreme are the behavioral scientists represented
most typically by B. F. Skinner, principal inventor of the teaching
machine. Skinner's definition of behavior is activity which can be
seen or measured. If there is no observable change in activity, then
no behavior change occurs. Since learning means changing behavior,
learning can thus be measured by measuring the rate and direction
of behavior change.

This position implies that the behavior of persons is a result of
shaping forces in the environment, including other people and
teaching. While there is room for some theoretical dispute here, as a
practical approach to management this approach meets business
demands for theory (proposed explanations of actuality) better
than the needs concept.

- Behavior is what is asked for and rewarded in business.
- The internal workings of attitudes and motivations, along
  with the individual's personality, are left to his own management, together with his privacy and his right to refuse to
  succeed or fail.
- The presumption that the individual will respond situationally
  to the shaping influences in different environments leaves him
  free to seek out the kinds of situations outside the displeasing
  job where his behavior is more personally suited to his attitudes.
- Measurable behavior is consistent with the measurable rewards basic to the business system.
- Attitudes often *follow* behavior where such behavior is attended by feedback of success and adequacy at the time it
  emerges.

In short, the individual at work can do his job well, and be paid and promoted for doing so, and retain his personal privacy into the bargain. He is paid for the result of certain behavior, and his behavior can be controlled on the job.

Is Man a Machine?

This bald statement of the Skinnerian position as it might be considered in business strikes many as rather cold. Is there no validity, then, to the "needs theory" approach to management? To be sure there is. The fact that the Skinnerian type of behavioral measurement is the epitome of modern science while the "needs theory" is more Aristotelian and speculative, doesn't rob the latter of its usefulness, and even of its necessity. The world is not a godless, materialistic sty, and matters of the spirit and personality are still considered to be relevant to the work situation.

Thus, the needs approach is of the utmost importance in the overall management of business enterprises. It should be the basis of the total management posture toward the organization. Policy, procedure, and rules and regulations rooted in soundly thought out, if scientifically imprecise, theories, have great value. The pursuit of equity, justice, fairness, and ego support, and the style of personal direction that Rensis Likert has called "supportive" (i.e., ego building) may be impossible of measurement by many scientific standards, but they have an epidemiological value in treating the gross ills of organizational behavior. The manager who assumes the hard-nose posture because of dissatisfaction with the lack of precision in the needs theory may find himself failing to achieve organizational objectives as he becomes bogged down in union troubles, turnover of key personnel, excessive attention to squabbles, and the diversion of management and staff attention from organizational goals to personal vendettas.

Once such policies and procedures have been applied, however, performance can be sharpened by the shaping processes of Skinner and the more precise measures of individual behavior.

CHAPTER II

Relating Salary Administration to Management By Objectives

Wealth is not without its advantages, and the case to the contrary, although it has often been made, has never proved widely persuasive.

—JOHN KENNETH GALBRAITH

A system of managing which doesn't purport to cope with the practical problems of salary administration really isn't adequate as a system. In moving managers to behave in ways that will achieve company goals, the salary administration policies of the firm can function either to reinforce certain kinds of behavior or, on the other hand, to extinguish desired behavior, if they are wrongly conceived or improperly applied.

Salary administration at the managerial level in American companies is not necessarily applicable to companies elsewhere. There are some basic articles of faith about the purposes of management compensation in our country, and in our time, that differ from the ideas about salary in other countries, or in other times.

In modern Europe, for example, it is not uncommon for all

wages and salaries to be so closely regulated by the government that any possible incentive effects are minimized. In certain countries, such as India, the paramount concept of wage and salary administration is the necessity of the employee. As Indian employees say, "The company is my father." Additions to the family, or increased expenses, are often considered rightful bases for increases in pay.

Salary Administration as Incentive

The accompanying diagram (Figure 11-1), indicates the scope of salary administration under the management-by-objectives system of managing.

1. It begins with the company's achievement of economic success, which generates the funds available for salary increases. Obviously, if the firm is steadily losing money this sum will be less than if operations had been financially successful.

2. The distribution of these funds among the company's various departments is made by top-management judgment of the relative contribution of the respective departments as measured by their results. This distribution of relative amounts among departments requires that measures of organization performance be established in advance for each major segment of the business.

3. Within the respective departments, the total amount available for salary increases is distributed among the individual members on the basis of:

    a. The formal job evaluation system.

    b. Statements of performance against goals as worked out between the subordinate and his superior for the period or periods since the last salary review.

The Procedures in Wage and Salary Administration

Part 3(a) of this larger system of using pay for incentive purposes deserves close scrutiny, and a more detailed explanation of the procedures used. These procedures, which have been well spelled out in the literature of personnel administration, constitute

Figure 11-1

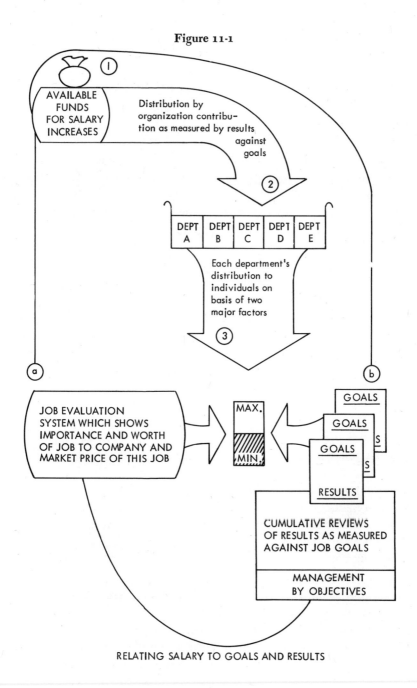

① AVAILABLE FUNDS FOR SALARY INCREASES

Distribution by organization contribution as measured by results against goals

②

| DEPT A | DEPT B | DEPT C | DEPT D | DEPT E |

Each department's distribution to individuals on basis of two major factors

③

Ⓐ

JOB EVALUATION SYSTEM WHICH SHOWS IMPORTANCE AND WORTH OF JOB TO COMPANY AND MARKET PRICE OF THIS JOB

MAX.

MIN.

Ⓑ

GOALS

GOALS

GOALS

S

S

RESULTS

CUMULATIVE REVIEWS OF RESULTS AS MEASURED AGAINST JOB GOALS

MANAGEMENT BY OBJECTIVES

RELATING SALARY TO GOALS AND RESULTS

a logical sequence that makes it a sub-system of the entire compensation process.

As may be seen from the accompanying diagram (Figure 11-2), the process of salary administration has six major phases:

1. The initial building-block for salary administration begins with a person at work. This includes the many activities he performs, the responsibilities he assumes, and the behavior he exhibits. The clerk, the machinist, the typist, the sweeper pushing a broom, or the salesman making a presentation to a customer, are all examples of this first figure. Their work is widely different, but we hope to measure its worth by a standard scale that provides internal equity and also keeps the company competitive with other employers of the same kinds of workers.

2. To reduce this multifarious array of activities to a common dimension of measurement, we prepare *job descriptions* for each position (or for benchmark positions that are typical of a family of occupations). These job descriptions use a common language and common patterns of description to delineate the work performed in each job. Thus, measurable statements of likenesses and differences among the jobs described are achieved.

3. The next step is to weigh the job descriptions to determine the relative worth of the jobs described. This process, which is known as *job evaluation,* consists of matching the respective job descriptions against certain yardsticks or measures of differences and similarities in content. Among the more common systems of job evaluation are ranking of jobs by subjectively judging their relative worth to the firm; use of a point scoring system that assigns numerical weights to certain factors that have been determined as having worth to the firm; comparison of the relative weight of factors that might be present in the job, and so on. All such methods require two ingredients:

a. Descriptions of the jobs being done.

b. Some kind of measuring scale to determine the relative weight of the content of the jobs as described.

4. After being evaluated, the jobs are arrayed in stratified ranks, called job grades. For example, the labor grades may ascend by modular blocks with all jobs evaluated as having 165-200 points

Figure 11-2

THE PROCESS OF JOB EVALUATION AND SALARY ADMINISTRATION

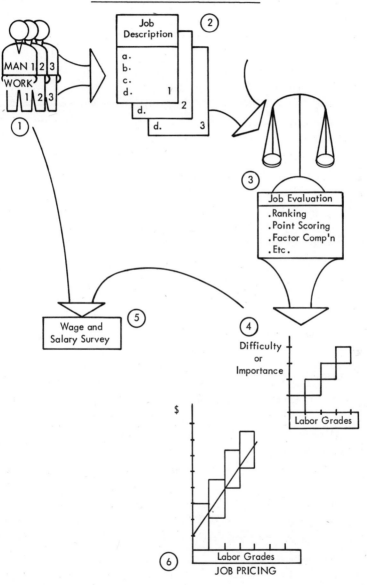

being placed in labor grade I; jobs with 201-235 points in labor grade II, and so on. The aim of this classification system is to insure equity in pay for different jobs, in different locations, or in different sections of the same location.

5. Internal equity isn't the only factor to be considered however. Our employees may be equitably paid in relation to one another, but over or underpaid in relation to the general market for their skills. Hence we must see how our rates compare with those prevailing in the labor market from which we hire our people. To make this comparison, we ask other employers to provide us with the dollar rates for jobs that are similar to ours. This industry or community survey assures us that we aren't overpaying any single occupation, and also that we aren't being non-competitive to the degree that we shall not be able to hire enough qualified people to staff our positions.

6. Finally, labor grades are matched against the market prices for the various jobs in the company and the jobs are priced in current dollars. The community or industry average for these positions is shown as a sloping curve, being considered as a *range* with a minimum and a maximum salary. Whether the firm should pay above or below the community curve, or merely match it, is a top management policy decision based upon such factors as the company's profit position, the labor market it operates in, or other reasons.

The end result of this procedure is a system that offers comparable pay for comparable work done, with due attention to length of service, performance levels, and the firm's competitive posture.

At periodic intervals, an employee's salary is reviewed to determine whether he should be moved toward the maximum for his range. The basis for this decision is the performance appraisal system.

Ordinarily for managers, the system should provide for performance to be reviewed more often than salary, with cumulative performance results forming the basis for increases in salaries within the grade and range.

Such is the sequence of standard administration procedures. For higher-level executives, however, some further considerations have to be borne in mind.

How Much Is an Executive Worth?

The financial rewards of top executives cannot be determined by the same criteria used to compensate other employees—not even key scientists or other professionals. The executive's job is, in many ways, unique and thus not susceptible to standard valuation. Essentially, the corporate manager is a risk bearer who assumes the responsibilities of ownership without its benefits. The rewards of top executives must stimulate them to run their businesses with maximum efficiency and profit. Ultimately, their remuneration should be related to the benefits stockholders, workers, and the general public derive from skillful management.

As we pointed out at the beginning of this book, the old-style capitalism of Adam Smith has vanished. With it has gone the automatic reward for risk enjoyed by the nineteenth-century entrepreneur.

It was easy for this man to reward himself. He took what was left over after all the bills had been paid. He didn't even have to share the profit with the income-tax man. If he wanted to spend the money, he could do so; if he wanted to reinvest it in the hope of making more, that, too, was up to him.

But in our time the corporate manager has taken charge, performing the functions previously discharged by the owner. Yet, since the manager is not the owner, he does not have the free access to the till that the entrepreneur enjoyed. In fact, it's often argued that the corporate manager is only a highly paid employee.

Yet, if a top executive must bear the risks without hope of attendant gain, he is likely to manage the affairs of the company with diminished zeal and enthusiasm. As far back as 1932 Adolph Berle and Gardiner Means pinpointed this problem in *The Modern Corporation and Private Property.*

"If all profits are earmarked for the security holder," the authors asked, "where is the inducement for those in control to manage the enterprise efficiently? When none of the profits are to be retained by them, why should they exert themselves beyond the amount necessary to maintain a reasonably satisfied group of stockholders?"

The two economists concluded that if the incentive system is to work, profits must be distributed "either to the owners or to the control" (i.e., management). This being the case, in our own time of far-flung corporate ownership, profit incentives should apply only to management which creates the profit, since the stockholders are "merely the recipients of the wages of capital."

Anyone who has attended a stockholders' meeting is aware of the inherent conflicts between the corporate managers and the "owners." Thus no aspect of corporate life is more loaded with economic, social, political, and administrative implications than the question of executive pay levels.

- When is an executive overpaid?
- Should an executive be paid according to different criteria than lower-level employees are?
- How can executive pay become part of corporate strategy?
- To what extent are executive pay levels determined by public needs and interests?
- Is there a discernible relationship between the level of executive salaries and the profits accruing to stockholders?
- How large must executive salaries be to provide corporations with vigorous and skillful leadership?
- How do tax laws affect executive pay practices?

"There are only three problems in executive compensation," a member of a board of directors of a large corporation said recently. "The first is internal dissension, the second is litigation, and the third is public criticism." These three factors provide a useful framework for an examination of the entire problem.

INTERNAL INEQUITIES

In large companies, executive salaries are scaled downward from the salary of the chief executive. Surveys show that if the president gets $100,000, the vice president in charge of sales will get about $70,000, the vice president of manufacturing or research, $55,000, the vice president of engineering, $45,000, and the vice president of personnel, $35,000. If the president refuses to accept a raise, he may compress salaries at the bottom levels of the scale, especially if there are six or seven levels between the top executive and the first-line manager.

The problems don't end here, however. Psychologist Jay Otis of Western Reserve University, who specializes in salary administration problems, points out that within each department or division, pay scales are likewise cued to the remuneration of the chief officer of the department.

Consider the sales vice president who gets $70,000 per year, and the vice president of manufacturing who gets $55,000. In their respective departments, the salaries of their subordinates will tend to slope downward from their own pay levels. Thus, the manufacturing vice president may have reporting to him the manager of a substantial manufacturing plant who will earn, say, $20,000 per year, while a regional sales manager who doesn't even report directly to the sales vice president may get as much as the plant manager, though he has less responsibility and certainly fewer people to supervise. This arrangement extends down through the organization so that the plant manager's secretary is paid less than the sales manager's secretary simply because the salaries are arranged around different clusters. Admittedly, a rational salary administration system would eliminate such inequities at the lower levels of the corporate hierarchy. But, in practice, the salaries usually cluster under the department's top man, and this may create internal dissension within the company.

The problem could be resolved to a considerable extent, however, if agreement could be reached on a definition of the term "executive." Some authorities take the view that an executive is someone who formulates plans, reviews the work of others, and integrates the demands of various groups within a business enterprise. Others would classify in the executive category anyone who has professional, managerial, or technical status and makes important decisions bearing on profits. This definition would encompass such individuals as researchers and corporate counsel. Milton Rock, a leading management consultant, recently endorsed the latter view in a talk before the Montreal Personnel Association.

Dean Charles Abbott of the University of Virginia Graduate School of Business has proposed still another definition. He concludes that the executive is someone who acts in a way that gives him a unique role in the company and in society. He is the paid risk-bearer, which is different from being a paid administrator (who is, in reality, a high-level employee). The administrator is an expert solely responsible for the professional quality of his advice. The executive must make decisions, guide their implementation, and bear responsibility for the results.

The risk-taker must be compensated for his risk-assuming role, which was formerly incumbent on the owner. In the large company, then, individuals below the rank of *division general manager* cannot be classed as true executives, according to Abbott's definition. A division general manager is the lowest ranking official who makes decisions directly bearing on corporate profits.

Under this concept, a designer for General Motors, for example, is responsible for the quality of his work, which is vital to the future of the business. But only the company president, the executive committee and the managers of Chevrolet, Buick, Oldsmobile, and other GM divisions decide which alternative design will be chosen and put into production.

Salary policy for the executive group is quite distinct from that for engineers, market research experts, and others. All the latter are *vital employees,* but their salaries can be arrived at by standard procedures. Determining the salary of a vital employee is a matter of viewing his particular job against a set of factors that apply to all jobs—his grade classification, the condition of the labor market at the time, the funds available for salaries, and so on.

It is pointless to follow this standard procedure in determining the remuneration of risk bearers, because their functions are unique. *The executive must be paid for the results he obtains in terms of profit and growth.*

Let's consider the president of a small company manufacturing envelopes. Under his management, the company makes a profit of $1 million on $10 million in sales and an investment of $5 million. The president's aggregate compensation is $95,000 a year, though the company has only 500 employees. The competing companies in his field are doing one-quarter as well in terms of profit and return on investment.

Now let us compare the envelope company president with the top executive of a company in a different field with annual sales of $300 million and earnings of $3 million on an investment of $150 million; he gets only $80,000.

If we applied the standard job evaluation procedures to both executives, the president of the envelope company would be considered overpaid. Yet the president of the large company may not be worth his pay, while the president of the small company may actually be underpaid considering the results he is achieving in the envelope field.

Or take two division managers of one large corporation. General manager A runs a highly profitable small division which earns fifteen per cent on sales. General manager B runs a division with ten times as many employees, a bigger investment, and a sales volume fifteen times as large. Yet his absolute profit is only twice that of the small division, and his rate of profit ninety per cent lower.

Obviously we must consider other factors as well in determining the relative remuneration of the two executives in this instance. Is one man cruising along in a soft job where any manager of average ability could make money because of trade advantages, patent position, or windfall profits? Is the manager whose division shows a lower rate of profits faced with extraordinary problems of competition, costs, declining markets or other obstacles that would overwhelm a person of ordinary caliber, problems which he, through special ability, has partly overcome and, as a consequence, has succeeded in preventing them from causing sizable losses?

The case of many Eastern railroads is a pertinent example here. These carriers lose large sums of money on passenger traffic and earn large amounts hauling freight. Does this mean that the passenger traffic manager should be paid less than the manager of the freight department? Not necessarily. A more realistic approach would be to measure each man's performance against reasonable expectations under prevailing conditions. If the freight traffic manager doesn't take advantage of all his opportunities, this should be reflected in the size of his compensation or bonuses. On the other hand, if the passenger traffic chief reduces losses, even though still operating in the red, he should be rewarded for his contribution as measured against reasonable expectations.

It should be evident, therefore, that no simple formula can be applied in rewarding individuals for generating profits.

THE LITIGATION PROBLEM

Corporation and tax laws provide ample opportunities for legal troubles when a company, especially one with a board heavily dominated by its officers, appears to be self-serving in its compensation policies.

As a rule, the stockholder is a fairly passive animal when it comes to suing his company or its officers for excessive compensation. The stockholder is willing to be treated simply as a recipient of the "wages of capital" and only asks for a fair shake. When dividends are not forthcoming, the stockholders may unite into a militant, but, for the most part, ineffectual organization which badgers management at annual meetings. It is only infrequently that stockholder ire results in a lawsuit against management.

More often the dissatisfied stockholders simply sell their holdings and buy another stock that is paying a higher return. The thought seldom crosses their minds that they have bought anything more than an equity on earnings. Of late, stockholders have seemed to be even a trifle indifferent to this, provided management uses the non-distributed surplus in such a way that the value of the stock increases fast enough.

Another kind of litigation that might confront management is a suit in the tax courts by the Internal Revenue Service. Such suits are brought by the IRS against corporations who don't abide by rulings on executive compensation.

The most important legal restraints, however, are those affecting possible tax loopholes for executives. High salaries obviously provide little incentive if a sizable proportion of them has to be remitted to the tax collector. Accordingly, corporations are continuously devising executive compensation plans designed to mitigate the tax burden.

One answer to the problem of high income taxes is *deferred compensation*. Here, part of the executive's compensation is held back until he retires, when his income will be smaller and consequently subject to a lower rate of taxation.

Stock option plans permit executives to buy company shares at a price below the going market price as of a certain date. Since the executive is granted several years in which to pick up his options, he can often wait until a propitious time arises to buy. Or he may buy the shares and hold them until he can sell them at a sizable profit. Either way, provided he holds the shares for six months or longer, he pays a capital gains tax instead of the steeper income tax. At the same time, he has a powerful incentive to make the company prosper so that the value of his stock will increase and he can sell it at a profit. Recent changes in tax law, however, have reduced the time period over which options may be exercised, thus making this form of compensation less attractive than it was before the new law was passed.

PUBLIC CRITICISM

Public criticism is another important factor influencing the compensation of executives. This is mainly directed at the practice of granting top managers large bonuses over and above their high salaries. Typical labor union newspapers usually make a point of comparing hefty executive bonuses with the pay of workers. Such comparisons are especially popular at a time when contracts are being negotiated. Recently, the Railroad Brotherhoods protested that during the past year, while jobs of workers had been eliminated, the number of executive positions on Class I railroads, paying over $25,000 annually, had sharply increased. And in 1963 the *Detroit Free Press* headlined two stories: a statement by an auto company official that further wage increases for workers were considered inflationary and a report that large bonuses had been distributed to officers of the same company. Such stories impress the public, but how valid are the objections to the managerial bonuses?

The real test is whether the stockholders, the workers, and the public profit or suffer because of such bonuses. Few General Motors stockholders, for example, complain because twelve per cent of profits, after deducting six per cent of net capital, may be placed in a bonus pool and distributed to key officials on the "bonus roll." The "progress sharing plan" of American Motors extended the sharing of profits down to assembly-line workers, an innovation that made executive bonuses much more palatable.

Perhaps arguments for rewarding such intangibles as "leadership" can never be fully communicated to the general public. Thus public criticism can be expected to continue. The true test is whether the policy makers in Congress and the executive branch of the government will have the insight and the pertinent facts to refrain from reducing everyone's rewards to one common denominator.

Some psychologists maintain that people seek other rewards besides money. However, I haven't been able to get those same psychologists to expound their theories at a management conference for less than a $200 fee. As one wag put it, in motivating people, "money beats whatever comes second best by a substantial margin." For more than two decades now it has been fashionable to proclaim the death of economic man and to kick the corpse for good measure. Experience with executive compensation seems to indicate, however, that there is still some life left in the old boy.

CHAPTER 12

The Problem of the
Annual Performance Review

A thick skin is a gift from God.
—Konrad Adenauer

There is no special significance in manager-
ial performance being reviewed *annually*. The underlying value of
performance appraisal is the opportunity it affords to feed back results against goals in order to improve performance. This doesn't
necessarily have to take place at year's end, as if it magically coin-
cided with the rotation of the earth on its axis, like a pagan holiday.

It's merely convenient for some purposes.

For example, though money budgets and profits statements are
made annually to stockholders, they are also released quarterly to
stockholders and monthly to officers. Similarly, budgets for coming
years and estimated sales forecasts are made up by the years with
quarterly estimates as well.

Even tax bills are no longer annual events, now that payments
of estimated tax have to be made quarterly

Salary reviews are more and more likely to come at times other
than at some period based upon the rotation of the earth around the
sun. At higher levels, salaries may be reviewed only every 18 months
or two years. By contrast, the salaries of new hires in the clerical

ranks are reviewed after three months. Some salary reviews do fall annually, but this practice is being dispensed with in many firms.

Annual Reviews and Management Superstitions

A year seems to be the customary time interval for performance reviews but there are some definite dangers to be skirted in adhering to this schedule.

Many annual reviews as presently conducted lead to managerial superstitions, which have a distracting, or positively damaging, effect upon people's performance. That is to say, they lead subordinates into unnecessary and irrelevant acts based upon the false supposition that such behavior will bring about better reviews. This is the same pattern of behavior as that exhibited by small boys just before Christmas, and may be called the "Santa Claus" effect.

Figure 12-1

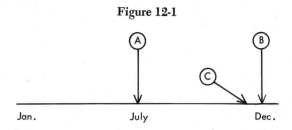

Jan.   July   Dec.

In Figure 12-1, the line represents a chronological pattern of events involving feedback to a subordinate of the boss's satisfaction or dissatisfaction with results. At Point A an action which the boss expects occurs (or fails to occur). At Point B the boss does his annual review of performance, at which time he takes the opportunity to lash the subordinate for his failure back at A. To the subordinate, however, recent event C, which is quite unrelated to A, immediately comes to mind as being the real reason for the boss's outburst. Here's an actual example:

A department head casually asked one of his subordinate managers to investigate a problem and write him a report. "No hurry," the boss said. "I'd like to have it in a month or so." The subordinate got caught up in some emergencies and wasn't able to turn in the report. By the time he thought of it again, several months had gone by. His boss never mentioned the matter again until the end of the year, about eight months after he had asked for the report. Then, in his annual review, he stormed at the subordinate for his laxity, his carelessness, his indifference, and other personal inadequacies.

What was the subordinate's reaction? "I'll never forget an order again?" No. The first thing the subordinate did was to race back over the events of the past few days and try to figure out what had happened to trigger such abuse. He finally fastened upon a minor episode two days before, when he had stepped aboard an elevator before his boss and the door had immediately closed and left the boss standing in the corridor. He recalled that his boss had been a high-ranking army officer. He went back over the interview and singled several references to his "desire to get to the top too fast." Putting all these clues together, he wound up firmly convinced that his boss had administered the tongue lashing simply because of the elevator incident. He thereupon determined never again to beat the boss to an elevator, and proceeded to pass this superstition along to his peers.

Now, as it happened, the boss hadn't even wanted to board the elevator in question. He was headed down, and the available car was headed up. What he couldn't figure out was how the subordinate could have missed a message as clear as the one he gave.

This story underscores an important point about the timing of the performance.

Prompt feedback is far more important in changing behavior than intensity of feedback.

In other words, if the goal is to change behavior, the feedback of evidence of success or failure in reaching goals should be instantaneous, not deferred until some procedural or ceremonial moment.

Under such a system, the annual review becomes a *cumulative* summary of the specific results previously fed back. Cumulative is simply another way of saying, "No surprises in the annual review." If the subordinate failed to deliver by some specific date in May and you as his boss never mentioned it, then forget it at the review time as well. Not only will there be no improvement as a result of your doing so, but there is also a distinct possibility that you will trigger a superstitious change of behavior that you can't predict.

Yet, adhering to the principle of instantaneous feedback poses two questions:

1. Does this mean that the boss spends all his time feeding back information about success or failure?

2. How do you avoid nagging and overly close supervision?

The Best Way to Measure Success

The answer to the first question is no—we shouldn't assume that the only kind of feedback that changes behavior is the kind that comes personally from the boss. Even better is the feedback the subordinate can *give himself* through measuring his own rate of progress and his own goal achievement. This he does by having his goals clear, and the many variables that comprise success, such as time, cost, quantity, quality service and results, under his own control.

The isolated plant manager who must read the daily results of his plant's output and other measures of plant performance should be able to know whether he is running a successful plant or not at the very moment he gets his reports together to forward them to headquarters. If he must wait for a return letter or wire to know whether he is doing a good job, he is being denied a real opportunity for growth in the job. Self-measurement against predetermined standards is superior to the boss's measurement of results. Self-measurement may, however, have a diminishing effect if there is no cumulative review at the quarter, half year, or annual period.

Such a system makes the job itself a teaching and learning situation for the manager, using the known principles of learner participation and immediate confirmation of correct responses. If, at first glance, it might seem to some managers too much of a release of control over operations for them to permit this self-measurement, closer scrutiny will show that it is, in reality, a more coherent and controlled approach to learning.

How to Avoid Nagging

As many young wives have found out, it is futile to nag people into changing their behavior. *Nagging*, in the sense used here, consists of punishing the subordinate for failure to achieve results he didn't know he was expected to deliver.

A boss is nagging, for example, when he awaits action, then descends either heavily or merely steadily upon those aspects of it that are bad, without having told the subordinates that such measurements were going to be made.

For the boss personally to pronounce success or failure judgments without having first established goals and measures of their achievement is nagging. It has only a slow and tortuous effect in changing behavior. Nagging can change behavior only to this extent: it punishes behavior the person didn't know he was being measured by. Hence he feels cheated and unjustly punished. He resents the injustice, and may rebel against the boss or the organization that has placed him in such a situation. To the extent, however, that he stops doing whatever it was that elicited the punishment, he has acquired a new kind of measurement and a guide to behavior. This can be achieved without primitive methods, however, and the resentment and emotional upset that accompanies this upside-down teaching method can be avoided.

The most favorable context for this melding of appraisal and discipline is that in which the superior views discipline as a teaching or behavior-changing process rather than a form of retribution. This process is identical with the procedure followed in using appraisal as a means of management development:

- The standards of behavior are spelled out specifically as a guide to action in the future.
- The individual's behavior is weighed against the standards that have been amply communicated to him as a means of letting him know the results expected of him.
- When an error occurs, the severity of the feedback is commensurate with the seriousness of the lapse, and should always, within practical limits, follow immediately upon the discovery of the error.

The Case for the Annual Review

In the business strategy of management development, the set of procedures known as "appraisal" is an important technique. It's also a difficult one, as many of us have found out. Briefly, the rationale behind the appraisal of subordinates by their superiors is that this procedure, well carried out, will improve the subordinate's effectiveness.

In procedures that aim at discovering the worth and capacities of other men and spurring them to greater effort, we know some things for sure, and in some areas we are flying blind. Perhaps it might be good to begin with the ideas that experience in administrative organization has shown to hold up. After this, we can explore some of the areas where we are far less certain as to the outcome of what we do.

Among our list, then, of accepted facts are:

1. In motivating people to be productive and creative in their work, we cannot rely on money alone. This conclusion is not only based on psychology but also upon economics. If we hire a young man fresh out of college at age 20, and plan to employ him until he reaches 65, there is a 45-year span during which we must raise and maintain a satisfactory pay level for him. This level of pay has as its floor sufficient productivity or creativity to recoup the costs of salaries and fringe benefits paid to him, and the other expenses of housing him at work, equipping him with tools, and providing him with materials. Simple arithmetic tells us that we shall quickly run out of money to recharge his motivational batteries.

For example, if we tried to give him a 10 per cent increase in pay each year until he retired, he would wind up with an annual salary of six figures.

2. While it might be possible in individual cases to maintain such a steady and large infusion of cash, this would be patently impossible for the company's entire work force. What then serves to motivate the individual who cannot be rewarded or spurred by money alone? This question becomes the important problem in motivation, and the economic fact that underlies the necessity of this seemingly sentimental question forces us into considering the feasibility of nonfinancial incentives.

3. In times of prosperity and full employment, we must rule out the negative motivation supplied by the employee's fears of losing his job, or of economic reprisal for less than excellent performance.

In dealing with skilled manpower, the emphasis moves toward some *positive* means of nonfinancial motivation, and it is within this environment that most of our modern systems of appraisal have been developed. Of course, these nonfinancial motivations must be combined with economically feasible financial motivation as well, but the nonfinancial motivations cause us more difficulties in management than do most others.

4. In good and bad times alike, we must face the fact that neither fear of economic punishment nor desire for economic reward can explain the full scope of human motivation. We may further assume, as Douglas McGregor does, that most people do have a desire to succeed, will work to achieve this success, and in so doing will exercise self-control, will accept and seek out responsibility, will exercise their creativity and productivity, and will work diligently to achieve corporate goals when these provide them with social and ego satisfactions. Assuming such things about people requires that we look again at our systems of appraisals to be certain that they are rooted firmly in the best understanding we have of human motivation.

5. Finally, we probably all know by this time that the appraisal process is just as much a reflection of the manager making the appraisal as it is of the person appraised. What the judge considers right and wrong is probably more important in many respects than the qualifications or actions of the defendant before the bar.

The theory of appraisals is that employees can be positively motivated to a considerable degree by their superior's following two basic precepts:

1. He lets his subordinates know what is expected of them—what constitutes good performance and what constitutes unsatisfactory performance.

2. He uses these standards of good and poor performance subsequently to let the employee know how well—or poorly—he has performed over a specified period just completed. This appraisal is both continuous and cumulative. The superior does it constantly during the day-to-day course of his administration, and he also accumulates these observations and sums them up in a periodic review.

On these things, all those who have thought about the subject are probably fairly well agreed. On many other matters, they aren't in agreement at all. Nevertheless this disagreement itself is important since it lays bare the fact that all is not perfect in the systems presently used for appraising subordinates, and that much more research and experience are needed before we can rely upon appraisals to do all the motivating of people we'd like to have them do.

Just how serious is this disagreement over appraisal methods?

The Battle Over Appraisals

Several summers ago the author and his colleagues were preparing materials for a film strip on management development. The film was designed to explain to a company how management development worked and could help it in the conduct of its business. The third section of the film was to be on the subject of *management appraisal*. To insure that the best and latest techniques were incorporated in the film, we invited a number of authorities on management development to sit down and confer with us on the subject and set us straight about what was right and wrong in management appraisal. The result, of course, was chaos.

Nobody could agree with anyone else—and this disagreement over philosophy and method in appraising the performance of subordinates continues without much letup among other spokesmen in the field. Douglas McGregor, Philip Kelly, Harold Mayfield, and Virgil Rowland are four of the principal protagonists. Rensis Likert, of the University of Michigan's Institute for Social Research, has likewise leaped into the fray. All these experts, it should be noted, deal with performance reviews as *annual* events.

In the modern corporation—the dominant economic institution of our time—this conflict is especially important. Thus, it's more essential than ever that we choose the successors to top management positions from among able and proven men possessing a sound sense of values. Practically all the people who will be running the great corporations in the future will be from the ranks of outsiders, that is, from the people who don't own the property they manage.

Most managers and top executives will work their way up the corporate ladder according to how effectively they comply with the demands of the appraisal systems that rate them. In our zeal for developing ingenious systems of appraisal, we must never forget this fact. Such conferences as these, in which "professionals" in appraisal rethink their systems of rating men, are vitally important simply because the resulting appraisal systems will be the vehicles through which some men rise in the organization and others do not.

The real test of appraisal, then, is not whether it makes people uneasy or whether it has full regard for the sensitivities of those who are chosen or not chosen; the vital test is whether the system allows the right men to rise and prevents others from doing so. Assuming, as we must, that the managers of the corporation in the future will be principally wielders of "power without property," as Adolph Berle has labeled them, the basic scale of rightness or wrongness of appraisal as a method of managerial selection will look something like this:

1. Appraisal must identify able men who have proven themselves competent and qualified for leadership in our business institutions through *performance* on lesser jobs, and have shown evidences of ability to assume bigger jobs.

2. The systems must be simple and the men must be easily *recognizable* as being the best.

3. The men chosen for leadership must have a high degree of *acceptability* to those who are left behind, since the latter will be ruled by those who were successful. As Gordon Rattray Taylor puts it, leadership today means that *"leaders must have the ability to prove their right to rule."*

4. Those chosen must have a proper *value* orientation for leadership in our society. In other words their qualities as total human beings, apart from those traits described on a form, must be suitable.

What Are the Technical Flaws?

We have all read and reread those volleys and thunderings about the problems appraisal presents. Many of them seem to center on the fact that the annual interview between the man and his boss during which the subordinate is told how others assess him is difficult, if not impossible, for the average line manager to carry out. Trained psychologists and counseling experts, who after years of experience, have failed to counsel people effectively, have honest uneasiness about what happens when "talented amateurs" try to tell their subordinates about their shortcomings—and more importantly, what they should do to improve. Yet the ticklish process of one man's telling another about his inadequacies is not the vital flaw in the whole procedure. The basic technical flaw in most appraisal systems is the lack of adequate *standards of performance* for the management job.

Let's look first at the subject of technique, and the four ways now most commonly used to set standards of performance:

1. MEASUREMENT OF A MAN AGAINST A LIST OF PERSONALITY TRAITS. Perhaps the weakest of all methods of measuring and appraising a man is the use of a predetermined list of personality traits against which the manager is expected to rate his subordinates. For one thing, as this book has frequently emphasized, we aren't at all sure what traits are necessary in a manager. For another, it's impossible for the layman to identify, let alone attach relative values to the traits he is supposed to rate his subordinate against. No doubt a trained clinician might be able through interviews, tests, and so on to ascertain whether or not a man is trustworthy, loyal, helpful, friendly, courteous, cheerful, kind, thrifty, brave, clean, and reverent. Most of us, though, aren't sophisticated enough to grasp precisely the meaning of such adjectives even with the help of the handy glossary attached to the chart, to say nothing of measuring these things precisely. Moreover, we can't do it much better in a committee than we can working alone. And even if we could, none of us is competent enough to be able to fasten upon the weak personality traits and then, in a private interview in the executive office, express our views to the subordinate with sufficient persuasiveness and clarity to induce any significant change in him. Because the standards are unclear, the appraisal will probably be faulty.

2. MAN-TO-MAN RANKING. Still another technique of rating is that of sorting out a group of people according to their worth and ability and ranking them from highest to lowest. Here too the flaws are of sufficient magnitude to cast doubt upon the system's efficacy. The standards again are unclear. For one thing, we know that in a sizable group of people only the very good and the very poor can

be clearly discriminated by this ranking system. The vast majority will fall into the middle ranges, leaving us with no option but to say to most people, "I can't find anything seriously wrong to complain about or wonderfully great to praise you for."

Another flaw in this system arises when we try to match up the ranking of one group with the ranking of another. We can never know whether the best man in Group X is better or worse than the best man in Group Y. In fact, it's possible that the best man in Group X isn't as good as the worst man in Group Y. The graduate school at Princeton, for example, is open only to the top two per cent of those in undergraduate school. As a result, their poorest graduate student is probably superior to the top man at Podunk U. Yet, Princeton reports that there are vast differences in abilities even among the members of its select graduate group.

In any case, you cannot expect to improve Mr. Adam's performance when all you have to report to him is, "You aren't quite so good as Mr. Baker, but you are superior to Mr. Charles." Parents learn quickly that invidious comparison is a poor method of stimulating their less accomplished children. Nor does it work with mature employees. If, therefore, you can't use it for improvement, it's certainly not a suitable instrument for evaluation. For certain purposes, ranking has value—in merit rating for salary administration, for example. But its limitations are great. Because the standard is "alikeness," it may result in a triumph of mediocrity in management.

3. THE MASTER SCALE OF MANAGERIAL PERFORMANCE. This is a scale that describes the general qualities required on management jobs or staff positions against which the performance of employees is matched. Here, once again we run into standards that are very shifty in nature. The hitch here is the assumption that we know what good management is. Thus we find master charts requiring a man to be rated on his ability to organize, to plan, to control others, to motivate and inspire his employees, to conceptualize, to integrate, to be productive, to be creative, and to delegate. It's a fairly safe assumption that these things are what successful executives do. We're less certain that the boss has sufficient discretionary ability to judge a man's ability in each of these areas.

Perhaps there may someday be a master scale of things that

every successful manager does. As yet, however, there is no full agreement on this point among companies or among managers. This system also requires that people who are perhaps not themselves good managers are asked to rate the managerial competence of others who may have more real executive ability than they do. As more able men are hired from the colleges or from competitors, and placed under the supervision of men selected under earlier and less rigorous standards, the chances are that most ratings of subordinates by superiors will be inadequate, because of the inferior knowledge of the boss of what constitutes good management.

In short, master scales of "what successful managers do" are often constructed by people without genuine knowledge of the management job for use by inferior people over superior ones. One suspects that such a system can hardly produce much that is very good.

It will probably be generally agreed that some progress has been made in the selection, placement, and training of managers over the past 20 years. This improved utilization of manpower must have placed many men of superior aptitude for the job under the supervision of many who have less aptitude for it. In short, in all too many cases today, experience and seniority alone are the accidental causes for one man's being the boss and the other the subordinate. Yet we persist in asking the boss to appraise as if he were just as able.

This improvement through the passing on of accumulated knowledge is evident in the colleges. Recently, Donald David, former Dean at Harvard University, told how one day he received a frantic call from the father of a boy who had been rejected by the admissions committee at Harvard.

"Why," the father protested, "I graduated from Harvard and this boy of mine is much smarter and more able than I ever was."

"Let's face it," the Dean replied. "Neither you nor I could be admitted to Harvard today, if we applied on the basis of our records through prep school."

In fact, a high percentage of college graduates might have a tough time today gaining admission to the colleges they graduated from in their youth.

4. MIXING APPRAISAL OF PERFORMANCE AND POTENTIAL. The rating of potential will be discussed in more detail in the following chapter. Here, it may be said that, in appraisals designed to serve this dual purpose, there's an overwhelming tendency to overlook present performance and rate the man high or low on the basis of an estimate of how far he will go in the organization.

Take the case of Dr. X, who is a researcher. Dr. X has a high IQ and a brilliant mind. Nobody can deny that he has potential. Yet when we come to rating him for an increase, we should ask, "What has he *done?*" Often this is an embarrassing question to ask about such a brilliant person, especially when, on further examination, it appears that he hasn't really done a darned thing. At this point we slide our system away from performance into potential and reward him for hoped-for things to come.

In some instances, the reverse of this is true.

Take the case of old Jim Smith. Jim is a solid citizen who managed to pull off a couple of deals that made the company a lot of money last year. Do we pay off during the appraisal time for these accomplishments? Only in part—because Jim isn't going anywhere in this company. We don't want to push things too hard, so we fudge a little on the appraisal and take off some points for his lack of potential.

SOME COMMON FLAWS IN ALL SYSTEMS

Whatever appraisal system is used, if the standards are vague, the procedure will suffer from one of two main kinds of flaws:
1. The halo effect.
2. The hypercritical or "horns" effect.

THE HALO EFFECT. The halo effect is the tendency of the boss to hang a halo over his rating of a favored employee. This can happen for a variety of reasons:

1. *Effect of past record.* Because the man has done good work in the distant past, his performance is assumed to be OK in the recent past too. His good work tends to carry over into the current rating period.

2. *Compatibility.* There's a tendency to rate people whom we

find pleasing of manner and personality higher than they deserve. Those who agree with us, nod their heads when we talk, or even better—make notes of our words—get better ratings than their performance justifies.

3. *Effect of recency.* The man who did an outstanding job last week or yesterday can offset a mediocre performance over the rest of the year by this single act.

4. *The one-asset man.* The glib talker, the man with the impressive appearance, the fellow with advanced degrees, or the graduate of the boss's own alma mater gets a more favorable rating than the subordinate lacking these often irrelevant attributes.

5. *The blind-spot effect.* This is the case where the boss doesn't see certain types of defects because they are just like his own. The boss who is a big thinker may not appreciate a detail man, for example.

6. *The high-potential effect.* We judge the man's paper record rather than what he's done for the organization.

7. *The no-complaints bias.* Here the appraiser treats no news as good news. If the subordinate has no complaints, everything is terrific. The fellow who pesters him but gets the job done is rated lower than the silent, solitary dud.

THE HYPERCRITICAL OR "HORNS" EFFECT. This is the reverse of the halo effect—the tendency to rate people lower than the circumstances justify. Some specific causes of this are:

1. *The boss is a perfectionist.* Because his expectations are so high, he is more often disappointed, and rates his people lower than he should.

2. *The subordinate is contrary.* Here the boss vents his private irritation with the man's tendency to disagree with him too often on too many issues.

3. *The odd-ball effect.* Despite all the lip-service to nonconformity, it all too seldom finds its way into practice when appraisal time comes around. The odd ball, the maverick, the nonconformist, get low ratings simply because he is "different."

4. *Membership in a weak team.* A good player on a weak team

will end up with lower ratings than he would if he were playing on a winning one.

5. *The guilt-by-association effect.* The man who isn't really known will often be judged by the company he keeps. If he hangs out with a frivolous crowd, or works for the wrong boss, he's due for some reductions in his rating.

6. *The dramatic-incident effect.* A recent goof can wipe out the effect of years of good work, and give a man a low rating on his latest appraisal.

7. *The personality-trait effect.* The man who is too cocky, too brash, too meek, too passive, or otherwise lacks some trait the boss associates with "good" men will suffer in his rating accordingly.

8. *The self-comparison effect.* The man who doesn't do the job as the boss remembers he did it when he held that job will suffer more than those whose jobs the boss is not too familiar with.

In short, ratings, founded as they are on human perception and judgment, must naturally be inaccurate. In industrial engineering, where greater precision can be attained, judgment is held to be impossible for closer than differences of 15 per cent in rate of effort. How much more imprecise, then, must be the judgments on the performance of staff men, supervisors, office employees, and executives?

Over and above the problems inherent in the rating process, there are other complications making it difficult to construct foolproof or even workable systems of appraisals. To name but a few:

In large, decentralized companies, a high percentage of appraisals must be done *in absentia*. The plant manager is rated by a man who may only see and talk to him once a month or less often than that.

With company growth and job transfers proceeding at such a high rate, a substantial portion of managers being appraised at any one time are likely to be working for men who haven't had sufficient time to observe them in order to make good judgments about their performance.

Many ratings have to be made on indirect information or insufficient observation. Except where close, daily, personal contact is possible, rating is often done on the basis of perfunctory knowledge, hearsay evidence, or results that cannot be directly related to the efforts of the man being appraised.

It seems to be abundantly clear that the solution to the appraisal problem is to devise better standards of performance for each job. The boss must sit down with each of his subordinates, work out an agreement with him about what conditions will exist if the subordinate's job is well done. Thereby, the two of them can develop some objective standards of performance. At the end of six months or a year, the mutually agreed-upon objectives are reviewed and the results the subordinate has accomplished are matched against them.

This eliminates the confusion over measuring traits. It obviates the necessity for man-to-man rating, because the man's work results are measured against his agreed-upon objectives. There is no need to define what makes for good "managerial ability." Nor is there any attempt to measure potential. Moreover, the system simplifies the problems of counseling because both men are discussing work results rather than the man himself and his shortcomings as a human being.

The Limitations of Management by Objectives

Yet, despite its obvious advantages over other appraisal methods, management by objectives isn't perfect—or even close to it. As a rule, those who install and develop the system understand it quite well, but this isn't so true of those to whom it's applied. To the subordinate, it often looks and smells quite like old-fashioned merit rating. And it has no clear-cut name that marks it off from other methods of appraisal. It's been called the "management by objectives" method of appraisal. It's also been called the "results approach," "performance budget and review," and so on. Moreover, at its best, it has certain limitations:

1. It can't appraise and completely identify potential. The system deals only with performance on the present job. Appraisal of potential must be done separately. To establish that fact, and to show how it contributes only part of identifying potential, see the diagram on page 190.

2. The system presumes that the man and his boss will together establish suitable standards that will serve the company well.

3. It implies that the boss understands the strict limitations on what he is supposed to do, and will refrain from playing God.

4. In action, it often aggravates a problem that appraisal should help to solve. It stresses results alone and doesn't provide for methods of achieving them.

What Values Belong in Managerial Performance Standards?

All the above problems and pitfalls in performance appraisal are, of course, familiar to anyone who has studied the subject. Time and again, however, this whole business of establishing standards of performance comes up against a problem that nobody has successfully solved as yet.

This problem is how to set fair and accurate standards that do not result in conformity. *The fact of the matter is that most appraisal systems used in industry today are based on standards that merely make it easy for the boss to fill out a check list and recite the results back to the hapless subordinate to force him to conform.*

This can hardly be called adequate for free men living in a free society. The result is often the creation of *neutral* systems of appraisal.

Neutrality toward some of the basic values upon which our business and social system is founded means that our appraisal systems labor mightily to measure one major quality of people—their *alikeness*. This is sometimes labeled conformity, and the end product is sometimes called the "organization man." Perhaps then we should think harder and better about how to achieve appraisal systems that will identify people with the human values and lift them out of the ranks into positions of responsibility, while at the same time carefully but surely preventing conformity-creative systems from gaining control of our business institutions.

Using value systems as a standard for executive appraisal is admittedly an uncomfortable step, but one that seems to be necessary if business is to overcome the deadening effects of conformity and repression of the individual. A system that merely polices alikeness and conformity does not take account of values. Its standards are neutral ones and deal only with performance. This could be dangerous.

Recently a manager, discussing his company's appraisal system, remarked, "The whole system is Machiavellian." Intrigued by this statement, the author looked into Machiavelli's *The Prince* and found that he had indeed touched on the subject of merit rating:

> A prince must show himself a lover of merit, give preferment to the able, and honor those who excel in every art.

Though Machiavelli gave no hints as to how this was to be done, there is substance here about which every manager might think. Obviously, from our knowledge of Niccolo Machiavelli and his philosophy we can read this statement as advocating the manipulation of people by the autocratic leader. Robert McMurry advocated the same thing a few years ago in an article in the *Harvard Business Review* entitled "The Case for Benevolent Autocracy." Machiavelli's phrase suggests, too, that simply rewarding performance is no indicator of greatness of spirit on the part of a manager, and that many appraisal systems today, even those which purport otherwise, are but thinly disguised means of manipulating people. It also points up the fact that rewarding performance alone through devising a clever system of appraisal doesn't accomplish all the ends we could desire from modern personnel management in choosing business leaders. If appraisals become mere systems of biological quality control designed to reject those who have lesser qualities of physical bearing, mental capacity, and social adjustment, they are as dangerous as Aldous Huxley's Fertilizing Room.

This love of merit, which gives preferment to the able and honors those who excel, is a minimum requirement, but it's essentially *neutral*. Achieving this first step is hardly worth praising oneself for accomplishing—even if it is being done effectively. The second step is the building of *value systems* into the appraisal of people for leadership positions. This, of course, is far less tangible, systematic, or possible of measurement. Yet, it's probably the essential ingredient in the whole process.

Not long ago the author read a chilling and unpleasant book which he would nonetheless recommend to every thoughtful person. It was the autobiography of Rudolph Hess, written in prison in 1946 in Germany while he was awaiting execution as a war criminal.

Between 1941 and 1943, as commandant of the concentration camp at Auschwitz, Hess had personally directed the execution by gassing of two million political prisoners. Most of these executions he had supervised personally.

Measured by many appraisal systems, Hess would have rated as an excellent manager. His production was outstanding. He followed orders completely, at the same time using skill and imagination in their execution. He was adept at the managerial skills of organizing, planning, and control. In such matters as quality of work, safety of employees, cost control and reduction, and engineering, he was superb. In his personal life, he was a devoted family man and regretted that his work kept him from his children and his animals, which he loved. He was thoughtful of his men. As he confesses in his autobiography, he did have occasional twinges of regret at the things he had to do, but it never crossed his mind that he could do otherwise than meet the standards of performance set for him.

The point of all this is that *technique* is always neutral, even the techniques of social science. Many appraisal forms used in industry today could be applied just as effectively to the dedicated Communist manager of a steel mill in the Urals as to the manager of a steel mill in Pennsylvania, and would rank both men equal on the same things. Yet, if we look at the value environments in which these respective institutions operate, we become uneasy that such an equality of rating could exist. It occurs to us that perhaps there should be some further standard for being a manager in a free world rather than in a regimented one. The value environment in which the executive operates is not neutral; it stands for something. Speaking of this value environment recently, Professor David Moore of Michigan State University said:

> The most important environment in which the executive operates is what we might call the *value environment* of our particular society. An executive is a creature of our society; he operates an institution which is a segment of our society; he is part of our ongoing history. . . . The decisions which he makes will have important repercussions throughout society even though he may see his decisions as affecting only his own business.

The question here, of course, is: *Where do these values come from?* Can they be built into appraisals?

CAN WE GET VALUE STANDARDS FROM TOP MANAGEMENT?

One of the most important forums for top management in our time has been the lecture series sponsored by the McKinsey Foundation. This is an annual event held at Columbia University at which the board chairman of a major American corporation delivers a series of addresses that are afterwards published in book form. Such outstanding business leaders as Roger Blough, Crawford Greenewalt, and Theodore V. Hauser have been chosen to deliver these lectures. Careful reading of their books indicates the keen concern of these men—a concern that is reflected in other contemporary literature as well—about excessive conformity among present-day managers and staff employees. What business badly needs, these leaders declare, is maverickism and nonconformity. Failing a return to these individualistic qualities, business will wind up with a corps of passive, dependent, and compliant subordinates.

Yet, if we study the appraisal systems in most large companies, we see the values of adjustment, compliance, and conformity strewn throughout the procedures whereby managers are measured, paid, and promoted. How do you suppose the store manager, or the plant superintendent adapts his value system—to the speeches of a board chairman whom he never met, or to his regular face-to-face contacts with a local boss armed with a check list that puts a premium on not sticking one's neck out?

CAN WE LOOK TO THE COLLEGES
TO BUILD THESE VALUES INTO MANAGEMENT?

Not for long. How much nonconformity may we expect so long as companies come to the colleges looking for "adaptable" young men? Not long ago, at the University of Michigan, we asked a group of campus recruiters what trait they most often sought in a college graduate. "Maturity," the recruiters said. Pressed to define the term, the recruiters explained that it meant that the student was "at ease with the recruiter, talked as an equal, and had no eccentric habits."

"I liked that boy," one recruiter remarked. "But he had a crew cut and I just couldn't bring him into the office for an interview because I knew what our executives would think."

IS PUBLIC RELATIONS OUR BEST SOURCE OF VALUES?

The speeches so many executives read are written by a committee of public relations ghosts. In one large midwestern corporation the author happened to be present when a young Ph.D. was instructed to prepare a stirring speech, in favor of individualism and deploring group behavior, for his president to deliver at a conference.

"Remember," his PR boss told him, "make enough copies so we can circulate it and get reactions from all around. Most of the group heads will probably have some edges they want knocked off, so don't let too much *pride of authorship* cause you to be disappointed when it's amended."

IS THE PRESIDENT THE BEST SOURCE?

In some organizations the president who sincerely feels the need for more individuality and nonconformity in the ranks is persuaded to take part in the appraisal system, even to the extent of doing an appraisal of his vice presidents. Sometimes, this is a purely ceremonial act, like that of the President of the United States throwing out the first ball at the beginning of the baseball season. In some cases, though, it's a genuine example of the use of appraisal techniques by a dominant chief for the purpose of bringing his lieutenants into line.

In such cases, though, it is more probable that the president is following the advice of his staff and using the form they have devised. When he is persuaded to use the appraisal system under these circumstances, it's most unlikely that he will swim upstream against it and arrive at any conclusions different from those built into it by its designers. One of the heroes of our time is the vice president of a large retail chain who was invited into the boss's office and informed he was about to be subjected to a periodic performance appraisal. Leaning coldly over the president's desk he grated:

"Look Max, if you don't like my work just say so right now without foolin' around with any form. I'll get on that telephone and in ten minutes I'll be merchandising vice president for the store up the street."

The president beat a hasty retreat, and appraisal was henceforth limited to those in lesser ranks, who had no such freedom to give vent to their tongues and their souls.

DOES MANAGEMENT BY OBJECTIVES BUILD IN VALUES?

Do we find less conformity when subordinates themselves set their standards of performance, working jointly with the boss? It must be admitted that no such favorable effect is likely to ensue if the plan merely provides a new design for the annual review. Rather than being democratic, such plans are often merely sophisticated forms of manipulation that become more acceptable to the governed because they have an air of democracy about them. Yet, self expression is more likely to occur where appraisals are based on results than upon subjective opinions.

This leads us to the conclusion that annual appraisals are part of the control mechanism by which a leader secures conformity from the lesser ranks. Their sole advantage is that, through more sophisticated techniques, the harness chafes a little less.

The biggest flaw in the annual appraisal interview is that the essential humanity of the person being appraised is, in almost every system, minimized or eliminated. Here's how Alan Harrington described the process in his satirical book, *Life in the Crystal Palace:*

> How can you come to know a man by means of the standardized interview, or nondirective questioning? The first pours your talk into a predetermined formal order; the second is designed through artful phrasing to *bring out* the job seeker, make him talk. Well, he will follow your order and he will talk, no doubt as you want him to. But curiously enough, with all these psychological maneuverings directed toward the discovery of a human being, an element of humanity is missing. You, the interviewer are the missing element—for the interviewer naively expects to receive honest personal answers to contrived impersonal questions.

The most damning thing about the annual appraisal interview is that the human qualities of both parties are set aside for its duration. It is not a communication between two human beings. It is *method* interviewing, a *collection of attributes*. When it becomes nondirective, the boss must pretend a concern he doesn't feel. If he does feel a concern, he must hide it. This sham must ultimately become apparent to the subordinate, so that the faked concern or faked neutrality of the boss is met by faked experience and faked attitudes on the part of the subordinate. The superior who conducts many such interviews soon loses his personality—along with that of the subordinate—when he's engaged in the process. After several such sessions, you find two actors talking past each other at the Psychological Corporation.

Take the common appraisal question which asks the subordinate to list for the boss his principal weaknesses. Who but a fool would hand his boss any of his real weaknesses on a silver platter? The question practically demands that anyone with his wits about him lie like Judas.

Or consider the frequent recommendation, "Praise first, then tell the man his weaknesses as you see them." How many times does a perceptive man have to go through this process before he learns to discount as sheer manipulative fluff the one thing he has a right to expect—honest appreciation of a workmanlike job in practicing his profession? As one man told the author:

"During the appraisal interview I just shrug off all the tripe he's putting out about my good work, and wait for the part that follows the BUT . . ."

Within the framework of the management by objectives system, the annual review offers the hope of avoiding these damaging effects, provided it is identified as a goal-setting meeting instead of an appraisal interview. Such an approach is positive in tone, looks forward rather than backward, yet, at the same time requires a summarizing of past events to lay the groundwork for establishing goals and standards for the future. Thus, the cumulative feedback of results attained is not eliminated, but takes place within the context of a meaningful behavioral purpose.

A goal-setting meeting must naturally take into account the significant events of the recent past that have brought the two men to the position they are now in. Thus the context becomes behavioral in the true sense of being concerned with "activity that can be seen or measured." The outcome is a learning situation, i.e., aimed at "changing behavior." There are no socio-psychological discussions of such matters as personality, motivation, perception, and the like. By starting with measurable activity and digging into its causes, the discussion evolves naturally along the lines best calculated to enable each manager to find for himself the answer to the key question: "What can I do, do differently, or stop doing, that will get better results in my management job?"

CHAPTER 13

Assessing Potential

Every soldier in my armies carries a marshal's baton in his knapsack.
—Napoleon Bonaparte

One of the most confusing aspects of appraisal is how to estimate a man's potential for advancement at the same time as one is rating his current performance for the purpose of improving it in the future. The belief that both these things can and should be done at the same time leads many firms to construct a form that is designed to serve both aims and is communicated to the individual at the same session. This kind of form often sets forth down the left margin a list of items to be checked. Some of these are clearly measures of present performance and others are personality traits or generalized character descriptions whose purpose is to aid in predicting the ratee's future behavior. This predicting of behavior on the basis of personality traits and generalized characteristics is usually regarded as constituting appraisal of the man's potential.

As a general rule it may be stated that appraising performance and potential at the same time is a mistake.

How Performance and Potential Relate

The relationship between performance and potential in the appraisal process is indicated in the accompanying diagram (Figure 13-1). Performance of a more than satisfactory nature is ordinarily considered necessary for promotion to a higher level of responsibility. We tend to trust proven men. Moreover, the policy of promotion from within could hardly be applied without some reference to a man's achievements of the goals that are presently under his control —achievements that are recognized by his peers as genuinely resulting from his own efforts and abilities.

Yet we know that simply being a sound performer at a particu-

Figure 13-1

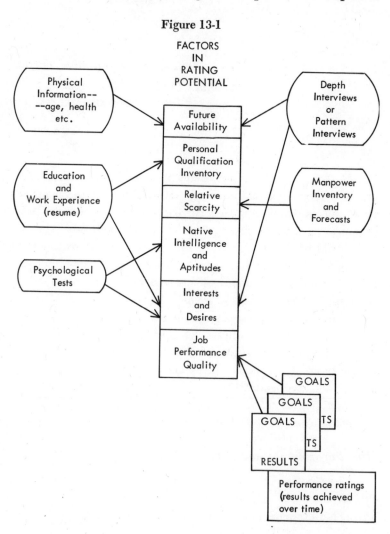

lar job doesn't necessarily qualify one for promotion to a higher post. Nevertheless, this error is often made. The best worker becomes a foreman, with little or no consideration being given to the question whether the same qualities are called for in the higher job, or the worker has the capacity to acquire the new skills that will be demanded of him. Quite often, no provision is made for him to acquire some of these skills before he takes over. Similarly, people in managerial positions are thrust into higher-level posts, only to find themselves over their heads. If discharge or demotion follows, this is a painful process for all concerned. But even worse is the situation where the man sputters along at a level of performance that is far below what the position could use, but isn't bad enough to justify his removal.

The Six Factors of Potential

In determining whether a man has the capacity for promotion to the next higher level, or for several promotions above his present position, a number of factors must be considered. These comprise the equivalent of long personal knowledge of the individual. The predictive process is inescapably one of managerial judgment—the judgment of one man about another. No single measurement has been discovered that will infallibly reveal whether a person has potential for greater responsibility or not.

The six factors on which prediction is based are:

1. The man's performance on his present and previous jobs.
2. His native intelligence and aptitudes.
3. His interests and desires.
4. The relative scarcity of candidates.
5. The individual's future availability for promotional opportunities.
6. His personal qualifications inventory.

Let's look at each of these six factors in detail. For convenience we'll consider No. 1 first, followed by Nos. 4, 5, and 6, leaving the knotty problem of personality assessment (Nos. 2 and 3) to the last.

JOB PERFORMANCE

The performance record of the individual still ranks high among the factors identifying a man for promotion. Poor performance in a series of positions may be some kind of predictor that he will not perform well in a higher job.

One large firm has a policy of rotating its younger men from time to time, so that a variety of managers can observe their performance. A single bad rating may only be an indication of a personality clash, or even that the individual is a better man than his rater. A series of adverse ratings, however, might suggest an inability to please any boss. If job rotation is to provide meaningful assessments, however, it must meet two major conditions:

1. The person being rotated must be given more than token work or observation duties. Rotation assignments that don't test the individual or threaten failure if he doesn't perform well are likely to be illusory because they never reveal the man's mettle in the face of real tasks that test his capacity to perform independently.

2. The objectives aimed at and the results expected should be explicitly spelled out and placed before the man as the major measure of his performance.

There can be no accurate measurement of actual performance without some standards in the form of statements of expectations. These statements must be given to the man before he commences his measured course of performance. The presumption, "A really good man will discover for himself what the job is," simply doesn't work, and places a premium on clairvoyance, or a similarity of temperament between man and boss. While such a similarity is fortunate for both, it doesn't especially serve the company to base its policy on the chance of its happening, since there will often be many man-boss duos whose personalities don't harmonize. If every such mismating results in the subordinate's being judged incompetent in performance, a tremendous waste of talent is likely to ensue.

For example, in one company there was a chief engineer who differed greatly in temperament from his engineering supervisor. The boss was a genial, outgoing, affable person, and the subordinate a tense, withdrawn sort of man. The chief often declared that he "didn't understand" his subordinate, and furthermore didn't think he was an especially good engineer. They seldom discussed the man's work, he said, because he felt that a "smart" manager would figure out what the situation was. The subordinate acted in accordance with his perceptions of his job, with the result that his performances

differed widely from his boss's expectations. Then a formal program
was set up. Together, the two reviewed the subordinate's technical
program and his major areas of responsibility, and then agreed upon
the ways in which he would be measured. The result was a marked
improvement in the subordinate's performance as his boss measured
it. This the superior attributed to "a change in the fellow's attitude."
In fact, his attitude had changed little. What had happened was that
he now knew better what was expected of him.

In still another company, difficulties were encountered when
young men regarded as having high potential in the field were
placed in positions where they could be tested against actual job
problems. Some of the young men were rated high by their bosses;
others were rated less favorably. A restudy of the results showed
that where superiors had defined the men's responsibilities in concrete terms, and had informed them in advance how they were to
be measured in their job, the newcomers received better ratings
than did those placed in departments where the boss had failed to
take these steps. Accordingly, the company instituted the practice
of informing each trainee of his goals and how his performance
would be measured before he was assigned to a department. As a
result, ratings rooted in the actual skill and effort displayed were
obtained.

RELATIVE SCARCITY

The suitability of a candidate for promotion may also be a
function of the other possible candidates, as well as the virtues or
shortcomings of the individual himself. During a period when young
men between 28–35 are in short supply, promotional requirements
for people in this category may be less stringent than at a time when
there is an abundance of candidates. If only three men are available
for consideration, selection standards are likely to be lowered, and
there will probably be a corresponding decrease in the quality of
selection decisions.

Relative scarcity cannot be estimated by looking at the candidates alone, though each should be measured carefully on all factors.
The orderly construction of manpower inventories and forecasts of
demands, matched against the total available supply, is of equal
importance.

The subject of manpower planning is itself a most complex one which cannot be dealt with at length here. Yet it is an essential part of the process of estimating relative scarcity, or the demand for talent against which potential must be estimated.

Figure 13-2

PRESENT ORGN.

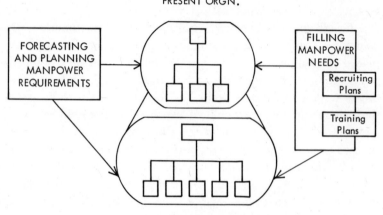

FUTURE ORGANIZATION

As diagrammed in Figure 13-2, the method of estimating an individual's potential as a function of the need for his talents is similar whether the manpower planner is estimating no change or growth in the organization, or foreseeing dramatic growth and change. Obviously the condition of growth alone doesn't determine the relative scarcity of certain types of persons, since that must also be considered as a function of quality changes in the organization. The firm that intends to move into new lines of business—perhaps with a more technical orientation than its present operations demand—may find that more technically educated persons must be brought along into management positions.

AVAILABILITY

The general factor of availability is used here in its broadest sense. Under this head are considered such aspects of the total situation as:

AGE. This is important in that it defines how many years the candidate can be expected to put into the proposed new job. Thus a candidate for president aged fifty, with presumably fifteen years more service ahead of him might be considered young. The trainee of twenty might be considered ideal if there is to be a long vestibule period before he assumes managerial responsibility. The length of future service of the younger candidate is an economic consideration, since the cost of hiring and training is amortized over a longer period of time.

HEALTH. Availability may depend on this element also. The victim of a serious heart attack, for example, may have unfortunately diminished his potential simply because he is no longer able to undertake certain kinds of work. Or a man with asthma might have to be ruled out of consideration for promotion to a plant location where the manufacturing process could aggravate the condition. This condition could be ignored, however, if all the company's work is done in an air-conditioned office. Diabetics are sometimes limited by their inability to travel without full meals, or the risks of traveling alone.

WILLINGNESS TO RELOCATE. Here is another element in assessing a man's availability for higher positions. The person who insists upon living in a particular region has a perfect right to do so. But this insistence limits his availability in companies that need to transfer their managers at will.

LIKES AND DISLIKES. Marked preferences or distaste for certain types of work ("I'd never take a factory job under any circumstances!") may also prove to be a limitation upon the man's availability in some instances. Here again he is within his rights, but his prospects for promotion may be restricted in consequence.

THE PERSONAL QUALIFICATIONS INVENTORY

The record of a man's education and work experience may be an important factor in judging his potential. For example, in certain chemical companies it has been decided that only chemists or chemical engineers can hold management positions in process plants and divisions. Without a chemical degree on his record, or its equivalent in experience, the man's potential is limited by the fact that his qualifications don't match the requirements of the situation.

Such a record is usually prepared when the man first joins the firm. Often though, it is not kept up to date. It should be supplemented by records of the successive positions he has held and for whom he worked, and any incidental special assignments that may have been given him. As each of these positions or assignments is listed, it should be accompanied by an additional line or two indicating the man's major likes and dislikes about the job. This provides a record of his interests and inclinations that may also have a bearing upon his potential for higher responsibility.

In short, the personal qualifications inventory should be more than a bare statement of the man's personal data, educational background, and work history. It should include details of the work performed, where it was done, salary progress, and so on.

PERSONAL CHARACTERISTICS

Finally, comes the problem of assessing a man's suitability for promotion in the light of his intelligence, aptitudes, interests, and desires. Here, psychological tests, combined with all the other sources of information and conducted under professional guidance, may be of some help. Some of the commonly applied tests for assessing men are those that measure the following characteristics:

INTELLIGENCE. This is usually a test of general information as measured by IQ. This test is often strongly oriented toward middle-class persons with a marked scientific or mathematical bent.

INTERESTS. Such tests show what tendencies the individual has toward certain kinds of activities that cluster around certain occupations.

SPECIFIC SKILLS. Tests in this category measure achievement in such individual skills as reading speed and comprehension, vocabulary, verbal reasoning, or number relations.

PERSONALITY. Such tests, usually felt to be the least reliable of all, deduce, from the executive's responses, his possession or lack of certain personality traits. If the test purports to measure specific traits, this is because the test designers have a feeling or some evidence that these traits are important for executive success. But as we have seen, the evidence that certain traits are necessary, or alternatively, highly unsuitable for executives is rather inconclusive.

Usually, a test should possess two major characteristics before it can be relied upon as a measure of executive potential:

1. *Validity.* This means that the test measures what it purports to measure. Another way of putting this is that success on the test turns out to be predictive of success on the job.

2. *Reliability.* This means that the responses can't be faked, and that each part of the test is so consistent with all the other parts that any attempt by the testee to make himself "look better" than he really is readily becomes apparent to the experts interpreting the results.

One common use of tests is to identify what kind of intelligence the testee possesses. Some people have great number relations ability, whereas others have non-numerical or non-verbal reasoning powers. If one of these kinds of ability is germane to the position under consideration, it can be uncovered and measured through such tests.

Tests themselves are always subject to testing, and the use of psychological testing scores in assessing potential is limited by several considerations:

1. Tests should be administered and interpreted only under the direction of a qualified psychologist.

2. Raw test results should not be handed out indiscriminately to lay managers, who might misinterpret the technical language in which they are expressed.

3. The measures of validity and reliability should be known by test users to interpret the results.

4. Tests comprise only one facet of the process of assessing an individual's qualifications for promotion, and should be regarded accordingly.

POTENTIAL VS. PERFORMANCE

The danger in discussing potential and performance in the same performance review is that the question of potential is likely to become so large in the discussion that it may never get down to the urgent matter of improving present performance.

Where potential is discussed, the following caveats should be observed:

- Don't discuss the man's personality, especially those weaknesses over which he has little or no control. "The trouble with you, Joe, is that you stutter," said one man to a fine subordinate. This curt comment caused the subordinate needless distress, since his speech defect was incurable.
- Center the discussion on specific changes the man can make in his behavior and thereby enlarge his potential. For example, tell him, "You might do well to learn more about the shipping operation," or "Perhaps if you spent more time with the accounting people, you would be better able to make cost judgments, Bill."
- Don't make promises you aren't sure you can deliver on, and if you make one, keep it.
- Don't compare one man's potential with another in the hope that the comparison will improve or energize latent energies in the laggard.
- Be honest and realistic in telling the man where you think he might go in the organization, without being especially gloomy or negative when you have to tell him, "I don't know."
- Always return to present performance and the necessity for doing an excellent job in the present position after any discussion of possible avenues of advancement.

Index